AMERICA'S DUMBEST CRIMINALS

FROM THE HIT TV SHOW

200 Wild & Wacky Stories of
Fumbling Felons, Clumsy Crooks, and
Ridiculous Robbers from the Hit TV Show

DANIEL BUTLER, ALAN RAY, AND LELAND GREGORY

Gramercy Books
New York

The contents of this edition were originally published in two separate volumes under the titles:
AMERICA'S DUMBEST CRIMINALS,
copyright © 1995 by The Entheos Group, L.L.C.
WANTED! DUMB OR ALIVE,
copyright © 1996 by The Entheos Group, L.L.C.

This 2000 edition is published by Gramercy Books™,
an imprint of Random House Value Publishing, Inc.,
201 East 50th Street, New York, New York 10022,
by arrangement with Rutledge Hill Press.

Gramercy Books™ and design are trademarks of
Random House Value Publishing, Inc.

Random House
New York • Toronto • London • Sydney • Auckland
http://www.randomhouse.com/

Printed and bound in the United States of America

A CIP catalog record for this book is available from the Library of Congress.

ISBN 0-517-20890-3

8 7 6 5 4 3 2 1

Contents

America's

DUMBEST
CRIMINALS

WARNING:
THE CRIMES YOU ARE ABOUT TO READ ARE TRUE.
THE NAMES HAVE BEEN CHANGED ...
TO PROTECT THE IGNORANT.

To
the men and women
whose portraits and photographs hang in the
lobby of every police station we visited—
officers who were killed in the line of duty.
Under all the portraits and photos,
the same quote was displayed:

"Greater love hath no man than this . . ."

Introduction

The plans were all in place. The phone calls had all been made, the faxes sent, the interviews arranged and confirmed. Now the crew was on location, ready to set up and videotape our hilarious yet revealing interviews with police officers who had encountered America's dumbest criminals.

Time was money. With every moment, hundreds of expense dollars were clicking away. And here was the assistant chief of police, the man who had welcomed us so cordially the day before, giving us the kind of stern look that goes with "You're under arrest."

"You need to speak to the chief," he said.

We were ushered into a large office. Before us was a huge desk, and behind that desk was a very big man. To us, he looked like more than just an "authority figure"—he *was* the authority.

The chief did not smile. In that office no one smiled. And no one spoke but the chief.

"Explain to me," he said, "what it is you boys want to do."

Something in his tone made me think of every lie I had ever told. I swallowed. Then I launched into a nervous, chattering "pitch" for the home video series and book project we were trying to produce.

I explained that we had come to collect stories from the officers in his department about dumb criminals they had known. I told of my phone conversations and faxes to his assistant chief. I talked a little about our plans for a book and for television pilots.

As I spoke, I noticed a small plaque on the bookcase behind the chief's chair: "Treat the media as you would any other watchdog. Feed it, water it, pat it on the head, but never turn your back on it."

I finished my explanation. No one smiled. The silence seemed to last, oh, five to ten years. Finally, the chief spoke:

"Son, you need to understand something. You see, I was the interrogator on the Ted Bundy case. I went through that whole trial with the media. Then Hollywood sent me scripts for their movies-of-the-week and they asked me to circle whatever I thought was inaccurate. I circled a bunch of stuff and they went ahead and shot it just the way it was. Plus, in the last six months I've had two abortion-clinic shootings and I've had the media climbing all over my back every minute of every day.

"So tell me again," he said, "why I should let your cameras in here."

I saw our whole project teetering on a toothpick. I swallowed hard, opened my mouth, and miraculously, words came out.

"Chief, I've got two sons, seven and fifteen years old, and they love to watch television shows like *COPS, Rescue 911*, and *America's Most Wanted*. They think those programs are accurate, that they show the way it is for cops and for criminals most of the time. They think the crime scene looks exciting, even glamorous.

"I don't think that's true. I think that even the term 'Most Wanted' glorifies the criminals—sort of like a rookie-of-the-year baseball card. And from the few interviews we've done already, I'm convinced there's not much glorious about crime.

"In fact, I'm convinced that you police officers spend 90 percent of your time dealing with idiots—or with people just like me who have been caught doing the dumbest thing they've ever done. That's what I want to show in our videos and in our book."

This time the silence seemed to last ten to twenty years—without parole.

No one smiled. No one spoke. Except, finally, the chief.

"Son," he said, his face relaxing into something like a smile, "if you'll show criminals for the coldhearted dumbasses they are, and if you'll show our police force as being professional at all times . . . well, then, we'll help you any way we can."

Over the next six months, this scene was repeated over and over. The stories were not all funny ones. With each officer that we interviewed, we felt the weight each one carries daily—the weight of pain and sadness and even fear. But police work, like any other stressful profession, is full of moments when situations take a turn for the absurd and when laughter seems as appropriate as tears. The most rewarding moments of this entire project came when the officers' very serious faces broke into broad grins and we all laughed so hard that tears came to our eyes. We hope this book shares a little bit of that laughter.

We want to make it clear, however, that in laughing at "dumb criminals" we are not making fun of the mentally challenged. We use the term *dumb* in the same way that great American philosopher Forrest Gump used the word *stupid*: "Stupid is as stupid does, sir!" We say, "Dumb criminals are as dumb criminals do, sir!"

Dumb criminals, in other words, are criminals who *act* dumb—people who opt for selfishness, ignorance, greed, or just plain meanness instead of using the good sense

God gave them. We take great satisfaction in showing the real and often hilarious consequences of such dumb choices.

None of the dumb crimes depicted in this book are still under adjudication. None of the criminals or victims described in this book are identified by their real names. All the stories really happened, but many details have been changed to protect the privacy of the people involved. The cops named in these pages, on the other hand, are very real. Their names and their stories are repeated with permission—and with deep gratitude. We wish them all the best as they continue to cope with the seemingly endless stream of America's dumbest criminals.

Never Mind

When Detectives Ted McDonald and Adam Watson of the Brunswick (Georgia) Police Department answered this particular home burglary call, they expected a routine report—missing TVs and VCRs, an empty jewelry box, perhaps a hijacked coin collection. But they were in for a big surprise.

As the two detectives drove to the address the victim had given them over the phone, they came upon a nice house in a middle-class neighborhood not far from their own homes. It was about five-thirty in the afternoon, and the victim had obviously just gotten home from work.

"The man whose house had been robbed was very upset," Watson remembers.

They could see where his sliding glass door had been pried open. It looked like an open-and-shut case of house burglary, one of several the officers had been tracking. But this victim introduced a new wrinkle in the crime spree.

"When we asked him if any belongings were missing from his home, he replied very quickly and indignantly that, yes, somebody had stolen his stash of marijuana. I looked at my partner in disbelief. We couldn't believe our own ears, so we asked him again just to be sure.

"Could you repeat that, sir?"

The victim's eyes got bigger as the cold, hard realization hit him. He had just admitted to a police officer that he possessed an illegal drug. He stammered for a moment in search of an out. There was none.

"Are you admitting to possessing marijuana?" the detectives asked. The man appeared to be frozen in time. He couldn't take the words back, and he couldn't think of any more to say.

"Sir? Is that what you're telling us?"

"I . . . uh . . . well, no . . . not really," the man stammered.

"Well, then, what are you saying?"

"Well . . . nothing, uh . . . I . . . oh, never mind," the man said. "Just forget it."

The officers turned and left as the man quietly closed the door, no doubt to sink into a chair and utter some expletives.

"We just left," Watson says. "Without the dope, we really had no case against the man. But we had a good laugh on the guy. And believe it or not, we've had several calls like that one."

The World's Shortest Trial

Officer David Hunter, retired from the Knox County (Tennessee) Sheriff's Department, told us this story of what might be the shortest trial in the history of jurisprudence:

At his criminal arraignment, the defendant stood before the judge.

"You are charged with the theft of an automobile," the judge said. "How do you plead?"

He expected to hear a simple "guilty" or "not guilty." Instead, the defendant tried to explain his whole defense as succinctly as possible.

"Before we go any further, judge," the accused man blurted out, "let me explain why I stole the car."

The judge's decision was made in record time!

Look Out! He's Got a . . . What Is That?

Our research has shown not only that some criminals are dumb but also that some use fairly weird weapons. Some of the oddest weapons used: an index finger, an egg, a bowling ball, a wedge of cheese, an artificial leg, a twenty-one-pound turkey, a hot-fudge sundae, a banana, a frozen sausage, a lit cigarette, a one-and-a-half-pound Chihuahua, an insect, a snake, and a toilet seat.

We can just imagine a dumb criminal attempting an armed robbery with a wedge of Limburger.

"Give me your money, or I'll cut the cheese!"

Positive I.D.

Detective Chris Stewart of the Brunswick (Georgia) Police Department told one of our *America's Dumbest Criminals* field reporters about a robbery suspect he transported back to the scene of the crime for a positive identification:

"We had gotten a call informing us that a woman had had her purse stolen from a shopping complex," Stewart says. "A short time later, we saw a man who fit the description given to us by the victim. So we picked him up and took him back to the scene of the crime."

Stewart explained to the suspect that they were going to take him back to the scene and that when they arrived he was to exit the vehicle and face the victim for a positive I.D. The man in custody heard this when the detective radioed ahead to the officer with the victim. Stewart said he had a man in custody who fit her description of the robber and they would be arriving shortly.

When they arrived at the scene, the suspect did exactly

as he had been told. He stepped from the car and looked up at the victim. And before anyone could say anything, he blurted out, "Yeah, that's her . . . that's the woman I robbed."

He has been given a new photo I.D. for his cooperation . . . and this one included a prison number.

Riches to Rags 5

Officer Brian Hatfield of Brunswick, Georgia, tells a sad story with a comical twist. He stopped a disheveled man behind the wheel of a fairly nice van that had sustained quite a bit of body damage. The driver had been weaving and was obviously a bit inebriated.

When Hatfield ran a check on the individual, he found several traffic warrants outstanding. So he brought the guy in for booking. The criminal didn't even have a dime for his phone call, much less the hundred dollars for bail. He called an attorney collect and then told Hatfield his sad tale.

"I won the Ohio lottery in April. Three million dollars."

"You won the lottery five months ago and you don't have a dime for a phone call?" Hatfield asked.

"I got the first installment, which was ninety-four thousand dollars. I went to Atlantic City and lost thirty thousand. Then I bought the van for thirty thousand, but

I got drunk on some really good French wine and rolled the van."

According to Hatfield's calculations, the man had frittered away most of his first installment, but not all. "What did you do with the rest of the money?"

"Oh," he said, "I spent the other twenty-four thousand foolishly."

D.O.B.

Officer Glen Biggs of the Knoxville (Tennessee) Police Department had a close encounter of the dumb criminal kind when he was booking a suspect on a narcotics violation. A simple transcript of the interrogation tells it all:

Biggs: "What is your D.O.B.?"

Dumb Criminal: "What's a D.O.B., man?"

Biggs: "When's your birthday?"

Dumb Criminal: "May 5th."

Biggs: "What year?"

Dumb Criminal: "Every year, man."

The two customers headed back to their pickup, oblivious to the uniformed officers and the two marked police cruisers in the driveway.

Drive Around, Please

J. D. Roberts has a colorful past. He has served as a member of the army's elite Delta Force and as a narcotics agent for the Drug Enforcement Agency. He has even worked security for some of Hollywood's top action-adventure celebrities. He now uses his expertise and experience as an instructor at the Federal Law Enforcement Training Center in Brunswick, Georgia. When we asked him if he had ever run into any dumb criminals, one incident immediately came to his mind.

One night Roberts was involved in a raid on a drug house that was doing a brisk business in marijuana sales. He and the other agents were dressed in black "battle" fatigues with "Narcotics Agent" stenciled on them. Local uniformed officers in marked police cruisers also took part in the raid.

Roberts and his team easily entered the house and apprehended the suspect. Several hundred pounds of marijuana were confiscated without incident. Within minutes, the officers were collecting evidence and finishing up at the scene.

As Roberts started out the front door, he noticed a pickup truck parked behind one of the marked police cruisers in front of the house. Two long-haired individuals got out of the pickup and strolled past the police cruisers parked in the driveway, then walked up to Roberts and his partner.

"Hey man, he still selling pot?"

Roberts looked at his partner, then back at the guy. "Yeah, he is. Just go around and knock on the back door."

"Cool." The two men nodded and walked on.

Roberts watched in amazement as the two individuals sauntered around to the rear of the house. Roberts radioed the officers still inside the house that they had customers at the back door.

The uniformed officers inside quickly hid while one plainclothes detective answered the door. The new customers asked where the old owner was, and the officer explained that the owner had stepped out but that he could help them.

They requested a fifty-dollar bag of marijuana. The officer went to the next room, grabbed a handful from the four hundred pounds of pot they had just confiscated and stuffed it into a plastic bag. The two customers were ecstatic. They thanked the officer for his generosity.

Roberts and his partner were still in the driveway, still wearing the black battle fatigues with "Narcotics Agent" stenciled on their chests, when the two customers headed back to their pickup, oblivious to the uniformed officers and the two marked police cruisers in the driveway.

Finally, Roberts walked up to the two satisfied customers and arrested them. The agents reconfiscated the dope and impounded the pickup—just as another prospective customer pulled up.

Roberts decided this was too easy to ignore. "We moved the two cruisers and started putting the impounded vehicles in the back. We made about fourteen more sales and arrests that night. By the time we were through, the backyard was filled with cars. It was the darnedest impromptu sting I've ever seen."

8 The Considerate Criminal

Working the front desk at a police station on a Saturday night is one of the most harrowing and maddening jobs imaginable. An officer can easily get behind in his duties when the phone is constantly ringing, prisoners are going in and out of the jail, paperwork is piling up, traumatized victims and witnesses are being herded through the hallways, and the miscellaneous weird people are wandering in. Bob Ferguson, an Indiana cop now retired, was working the desk on just such a night.

"A guy comes in around two o'clock in the morning and says, 'I'm wanted for robbery in Illinois, and I wanted to turn myself in,'" Ferguson says. "It just so happened that the desk I was working was located in Indiana. It was a crazy night, and there were a lot more pressing problems at hand than this guy. We were booking a rather violent guy on narcotics, and I had drunk teenagers throwing up in the lobby. Not to mention a prostitution sting that was processing about three hookers and five johns every ten minutes."

In the confusion, the officer blurted out, "That's all well and good, but I'm kind of busy. Either go to Illinois or come back at six." And at six o'clock on the dot, the man came back and turned himself in.

Bob Ferguson told the man how much he appreciated his punctuality " . . . then I politely booked him."

Taken for a Ride

Let's take a minute and flash back to the good ol' seventies.

Working undercover narcotics back then was a little more informal than it is today. A "flower child" mentality still prevailed in certain segments of the drug scene. This allowed for spontaneous and often funny moments.

At Purdue University, three undercover narcotics agents had been assigned to look for possible links to the drug culture. While cruising near the campus late one summer afternoon, they came upon a bearded hitchhiker with sun-bleached, shoulder-length hair. Peace signs adorned his Levi jacket and his army surplus backpack. Not having anything really pressing at the moment, the officers pulled over their Volkswagen van and offered the man a lift.

"Far out, man," he said, climbing in.

Soon the three of them were chatting with their new passenger as he babbled on about Nixon, Vietnam, and how much fun it would be to get high. Before long he had pulled out a fat marijuana cigarette.

"If you guys want to score really big," he offered, "I know just the place."

This was too easy. The agents eagerly agreed to take the man wherever he wanted to go. He'd make the buy, and they'd make the bust.

No one was home at the first house they tried. Their luck didn't get any better until the passenger remembered a dealer in another town. Would they drive the extra fifty miles to get the drugs?

"Sure, why not?" they said. After all, they were just out looking for a good time. Then, on a lark, they decided to pick up a friend of theirs, the crime analyst for their narcotics unit.

Now Roger, the analyst, didn't fit in with the rest of the group, who were all clad in leather jackets and sporting long hair and beards. Roger was clean-shaven, with a short, military-style haircut, and wore a tie and glasses. The passenger didn't seem to notice. He continued his friendly banter as he gave directions.

Before long the merry band of five was on its way in search of drugs, which the hitchhiker was readily able to supply. Finally, after a day of wandering from house to house, increasing their illegal stash at each stop, it was time for all good things to come to an end. Telling their newfound friend that they had some place they wanted to take him, the agents decided to wrap up the evening and drove him to the police station.

"This will be your new home for a while," the agents said to the passenger, who by this time was somewhat stoned and obviously flabbergasted. All he could do was shake his head as they explained they were police officers and that he was under arrest.

DUMB CRIMINAL QUIZ NO. 53

How well do you know the dumb criminal mind?

A man was sentenced to ninety days in jail for disorderly conduct, a fairly minor offense that carried a fairly minor sentence. While he was in jail did he . . .

- **(a) take a matchbook correspondence course in VCR repair?**
- **(b) whittle a replica of the White House to scale out of soap?**
- **(c) invent a straw that you could eat chili with?**
- **(d) plot and execute a difficult escape?**

Answers (a), (b), or (c) could all be rationalized as a good use of his time, but a criminal in Rhode Island chose (d). For eighty-eight laborious days he toiled over his plans, and then he finally accomplished his feat. On the next-to-last day of his ninety-day sentence, he made good his escape—for about five minutes. He was then re-arrested and sentenced to eighteen months.

10 Jumpin' Jack Flasher

Just outside Little Rock, Arkansas, a known "flasher" was at it again. Jumpin' Jack, as he was called by the local police, would often get naked and do calisthenics at his apartment window across the street from the local bank. Not only were his exercise habits offensive to the people who worked in the bank; local merchants also complained that Jack's jumping was bad for business.

Now, Jack was bold and a little demented, but he wasn't stupid. He would always hide his face in some way or pull the blinds halfway so that he could only be seen from the waist down. These precautions made it more difficult for him to be identified (especially in light of the fact that the police don't hold naked lineups).

After receiving a number of complaints one day, the Little Rock Police Department sent over one of its best officers to investigate. As the detective knocked on Jack's door, he thought about how hard it was to prove cases like Jack's. Without a positive I.D., such situations quickly degenerate to "my word against yours." Our detective decided to take a different approach.

"All right, Jack, who have you got hiding in there with you?"

"I don't have anyone hiding in here!" Jack yelled angrily from behind the door.

"The girls over at the bank tell it differently. They say they saw someone sneaking in here a little earlier today."

Jack opened the door. "They're crazy," he said. "There hasn't been anyone in my apartment all day long except me. See for yourself."

The officer did. He saw it all, from Jack's head down to his toes. Jumpin' Jack was finally arrested for indecent exposure.

Beats the Hell out of Me

Marshal Larry Hawkins of Little Rock has his own story about Jumpin' Jack Flasher.

"I had a run-in with Jack myself once," Hawkins told one of our *America's Dumbest Criminals* writers. "One day I was patrolling the downtown area when this skinny little guy stops my car. It was Jumpin' Jack. From the looks of him, he'd been worked over pretty good by somebody who wasn't messin' around. His left eye had a huge mouse under it, his lip was split open, and his face was all red, with a couple of knots on his head as well. He just looked like hell."

"What happened to you?" Hawkins asked.

"I've been beat up," Jack mumbled through clenched jaws.

"I'll say you have. Who beat you up, Jack?"

"This woman down at the Laundromat," he confessed in obvious pain and embarrassment.

"A woman? A woman did this to you?"

Hawkins thought maybe Jack had mixed it up with his girlfriend or something. So he put Jack in the back seat of the squad car and drove to the Laundromat. Through the storefront windows, the men could see several women inside cleaning clothes.

"Jack, which one was it that beat you up?"

"I don't know," he muttered. "I didn't see her face."

"Wait a minute . . . let me get this straight. A woman in there beat you up, and you don't know which one did it?"

"I told you, I didn't see her face."

"All right. You wait here while I go in and try to find out what happened." So Hawkins walked into the place. One of the women addressed Hawkins, "Officer, we are so glad you're here. A man came in here about ten minutes ago, pulled his shirt up over his head, and then dropped his pants."

"He wasn't wearing any underwear, either!" added another woman.

"So what happened then?" Hawkins asked, smiling.

One of the women continued: "Then the man said, 'Hey girls, does this remind you of anything?' And Connie said, 'Yeah, it does—it looks like a penis, only smaller!' Then she reached out and grabbed him by the hair under his tee shirt and commenced to knock the hell out of him."

"Yeah," the officer admitted. "That much is obvious."

"His arms were up over his head in that shirt," the informant went on, "and he couldn't do nothin'. It was over in about thirty seconds." Then she added with some satisfaction, "You don't mess with Connie!"

She was right about that, too, Hawkins thought as he looked at a substantial woman in the corner nonchalantly folding some sheets. *I certainly wouldn't mess with Connie!*

Hawkins got back in the squad car and told Jack he was under arrest for exposing his privates in public.

"Well, what about that woman in there? Aren't you gonna do anything about her beatin' me up like this?"

"I thought you told me that you didn't see who did it," the officer said. "But if you want to go back in there and see if you can figure out who it was, I'll just wait here for you, Jack."

"Uhhh . . . no . . . that's okay. Let's just get out of here," Jack said. He kept staring through the window at Connie, who was still folding clothes.

"Fine with me, Jack," Hawkins said. "Let's go."

Insulated from Good Sense

A narcotics team had a house in Indiana surrounded. With warrants in hand, they entered the house and searched the premises. The man who was making most of the drug sales was nowhere to be found, but they knew he was in there somewhere. The house had been under surveillance for some time.

Finally, the search took the officers to the attic. The place looked deserted, just like the rest of the house. One officer then noticed the right cheek of a pair of blue jeans sticking out of a roll of fiberglass insulation. At this point, an officer armed with a shotgun loaded another round into the chamber of his gun, even though his gun was already loaded. He was counting on the ominous sound of a pump shotgun being loaded to bring the suspect out of hiding.

Suddenly, the fiberglass roll started shaking and moving around, and the suspect was hollering, "Don't shoot! Don't shoot! I'm coming out . . . I'm coming out!"

But it wasn't the loading of the shotgun that had

33

prompted our friend to acknowledge his presence. Before the police knew it, their suspect was out of the roll and scratching himself all over. Every square inch of exposed skin was painfully red and inflamed from exposure to the fiberglass, and the suspect was so caught up in his scratching that he barely glanced at the cops. "I was ready to give up anyway," he mumbled.

That was one time a suspect was caught red-handed and red-faced . . . just itching to give himself up!

Suddenly, the fiberglass roll started shaking and moving around, and the suspect was hollering, "Don't shoot! Don't shoot! I'm coming out . . . I'm coming out!"

13 Going out with a Bang

Kerry and David weren't very nice people. Their idea of a good time was to get drunk and drive some thirty miles outside their southwestern city and wreak havoc on whatever innocent desert creatures happened across their paths. Mainly coyotes.

From their new four-by-four Blazer, they would either run them down or shoot them, or both, leaving their mangled carcasses lying in the desert. Sometimes they even set traps for the unsuspecting creatures, ensuring themselves sufficient victims for a day of demented sport.

Yes, the whole thing was sickening and deplorable. But there finally came a day when one small coyote managed to get in a little payback.

Our two sickos had removed a coyote from their trap and taped two sticks of dynamite to its body. Then they lit the fuses and turned the coyote loose.

Scared, confused, and panicked, the hapless creature ran . . . for about ten feet. Then it turned and ran straight back toward its tormentors, the lit dynamite still hissing at its side. Kerry and David ran. The coyote followed. It would rush one way, zig and zag, then chase after the other guy. Finally, the coyote ran for the nearest cover, which was a five-by-eleven-foot shaded area—right under the new Blazer.

The situation had quickly turned from bad to worse. The terrible two were now the ones scared, confused, and panicked. And they, like their little victim, were helpless. They couldn't chase him off. They couldn't drag him out. They couldn't even get near him. In fact, they had to run even faster now . . .

Kaboom! Bye-bye, Blazer.

Dumbfounded, the two ghoulies were suffering the consequences of their evil. They were thirty miles from home and stranded in the middle of the desert. No guns, no beer, no water, no whatever else they had brought with them—not to mention the loss of a twenty-thousand-dollar vehicle.

When the two were finally rescued and the investigation completed, the two faced charges of animal cruelty and other violations against nature. And once the truth was out, the insurance company refused to cover the Blazer.

It wasn't enough. But that little coyote, although doomed, had at least managed to give them a small taste of what they deserved.

A Large Naked Anchovy and Pepperoni

Police in Indiana arrested a man after an odd crime spree. It seems he dreamed of being a pizza delivery boy, so he decided he'd audition for the part. Police got the call when he went through an entire apartment complex knocking on doors—without a pizza, and wearing only a baseball cap.

Police arriving on the scene gave chase, and the would-be delivery man fled, only to injure himself as he attempted to jump over a fence. He was, shall we say, arrested and booked in thirty minutes . . . or less.

"Not by the Hair of My Chinny-Chin-Chin!"

Charlie Hackett, chief of police in Kokomo, Indiana, tells this story about dumb criminals determined to live high on the hog:

"Someone called in a complaint about some rustling going on out in the country. My partner and I were working organized crime at the time, but we were the only ones on duty, so we had to go. We found that this farmer had been losing big time—twenty-five or thirty hogs in all—but not all at once. Those hogs had been disappearing one at a time, one a night. And each time the rustlers had managed to take the whole pig. The farmer had found blood, but no carcasses."

Hackett and his partner staked out the area the next night. Before long, they saw a big station wagon rolling down a little lane near the hog pens. Three or four men got out. The officers used night lenses to watch the suspects walk down the lane toward the hog pens. Then the commotion started.

"They were running," Hackett remembers, "and the hogs were running. Then one of the guys pulled out a .22-caliber rifle and popped one of the hogs. He shot again, and the hog went down.

"Well, we backed off at that point, knowing they would have to come back down the lane with the hog they had shot. So we're sitting there waiting for them to get onto the highway so we can stop them. Sure enough, they came zipping down. We pulled them over."

The two officers approached the vehicle and peered inside, expecting to catch the rustlers red-handed. But all they saw were two men in the front seat, three men in the back—and no sign of a recently deceased hog.

One of the officers peered into the rear of the station wagon. "Nothing back there but an old seat," he said. Then they looked more closely and realized it was the backseat of the station wagon. The officers asked the men in the backseat to get out.

"Now, it didn't look too bad," Hackett says. "There was a seat cover over what appeared to be the backseat. One of our guys reached in and pulled off the cover."

It wasn't a seat at all. It was a very large, very dead hog. "We don't know how they did it, how they got that hog into the backseat—it must have weighed around five hundred pounds."

But that's not the end of our little pig tale.

Those hogs had been disappearing one at a time, one a night.

"Later on, we got a search warrant to go back to the house where one of these guys lived, and we found a small, live pig this guy had previously taken. We kept her for evidence, and one of our officers took her home to keep for the trial. By the time the trial came around, however, the officer had grown quite fond of the pig. He even had her paper-trained! The 'evidence' remained at the officer's home as a pet until she weighed about four hundred pounds, then she moved to a local farm."

Presumably, she never had to serve double duty as the backseat of a station wagon.

Junior Meets the Sandman

Officer Steve Turner of the Metropolitan Nashville Police Department had little trouble apprehending this tired, dumb criminal.

As homeowner Loretta Davin placed the last suitcase in the trunk of her car, she had no idea she was being watched. Twenty-six-year-old Fred "Junior" Williams, a small-time house burglar with a keen eye for opportunity, had been observing Davin for twenty minutes or so. Junior knew she was about to leave, and from the amount of luggage she was taking, he knew she would probably be gone for at least a couple days. Junior smiled as the car pulled out of the driveway, turned the corner at the end of the street, and disappeared.

Breaking in through a side door unnoticed was easy for our burglar. That's what he did for a living. And with the homeowner safely out of the way, this promised to be a stress-free operation.

Ah, life is good, thought Junior as he shook a pillow from its case. He then began a leisurely stroll through the house, filling his pillowcase with whatever he decided to take. There was some jewelry, some cash hidden under the mattress, the VCR—yes, life was good. This job was a piece of cake.

Hmmm . . . piece of cake. That sounded pretty good to Junior. He hadn't had lunch, and by now he had worked up quite an appetite rifling through the house. He decided to see what the kitchen had to offer.

Well, all right! The lady of the house hadn't bothered to clean out the fridge before she left. Junior found some nice chicken salad and a loaf of bread, a few carrot sticks, some potato chips, and some chocolate milk. *Hey, may as well put it on a tray, kick back, and catch a little TV.*

So that's just what Junior did. He carried the tray to the nightstand next to the bed, climbed in, clicked on the tube, and ate his lunch. But after all that hard work and that good meal, the bed was just too comfortable. The sandman came a-callin' on Junior, and soon he was out like a light.

Meanwhile, Loretta Davin had arrived at her office and learned that her business trip had been postponed. After being gone only three hours instead of three days, she returned home to find her side door broken open. Gripped with fear, she phoned the police from her car phone.

Turner was one of the first officers to arrive on the scene. Here's how he described it:

"As we entered the home, it was obvious that a burglary had occurred. Drawers were pulled out, closet doors stood wide open, and the place looked as if it had been ransacked. With weapons drawn, we cleared each room. As we got near the bedroom, I could hear voices, so we approached very cautiously. The television was still on. And there, all sprawled out, lay Junior, sleeping like he was in his own bed. The tray was there on the nightstand with some food still left on it, and the pillowcase of loot was sitting next to it.

"What a picture! We had had dealings with Junior before, so we all knew who he was. So we just kind of quietly encircled the bed and yelled, on cue, 'Junior! Wake up!' He did, and the look on his face was hysterical. We arrested him and took him to jail for breaking and entering, burglary, and sleeping on the job!"

Junior's short nap turned into a long stretch.

Write On!

"I've got another story for you," Detective Ted McDonald told us at a recent barbecue for *America's Dumbest Criminals* personnel in Brunswick, Georgia. "Adam Watson and I had to serve a warrant for cashing a stolen check on a man that lived here in Brunswick. I remember it because of the heat that day. It must have been a hundred. In fact, it was so hot that I saw two dogs fighting over a tree."

He smiled.

"As we arrived at the man's house and began to go up on the front porch, a dog starts barking. About this time a man comes from around the back of the house to see what the dog is barking at. It was us."

"Robert Norton?" the officers asked the man.

"Yeah, I'm Robert Norton. What can I do for you guys?"

"Mr. Norton, we have a warrant for your arrest for receiving and cashing a stolen check."

"Nah . . . you've got the wrong man." he said, shaking his head. "I never cashed a stolen check in my life. What makes you guys think I did something like that?"

"Well sir," Officer McDonald said, holding up the canceled check from the bank. "You forged the name the check was in on the front. But on the back, when you endorsed it, you signed your *real* name. And you provided the teller with your driver's license, complete with your current address."

"You weren't thinking too clearly at that moment, were you?" Watson asked.

"Let me see that check," the man said. He looked it over pretty good, front and back. Then he shook his head in disbelief and frustration.

"I'd never done anything like this before," he told the two detectives. "I guess when she asked me for my I.D. I just went into check-cashing mode. I can't believe I did that . . . pretty dumb, huh?"

"Pretty dumb," the officers echoed in unison. "Let's go."

18 Go Directly to Jail

It was a late Thursday afternoon in a Florida panhandle locale when two young off-duty detectives in plain clothes were approached by a local drug dealer as they sat and talked over a cup of coffee. Not only were they off the clock; they were also out of their jurisdiction, just on the other side of the county line.

"S'up dudes?" the dealer bantered.

"Not much, man. What's up with you?"

"Ain't no thang. Y'all looking for a little somethin' for tonight?"

"Might be," the detectives answered. "Depends on what we find."

"Well, look no further—the Candy Man's here," he announced with pride of title on his face. "How's two hundred dollars sound for an eight ball?" (An eight ball is 3.5 grams of cocaine.)

"That sounds real good if it's the right thing."

"Oh, it's the right thing all right. That's why they call me the Candy Man, 'cause my deals are so sweet!"

"Sounds good," one of the officers repeated. "In fact, we'd probably want to do a couple of eight balls right now, only at the moment we don't have that much cash with us. But if we could take a little ride over to our office, I could get some money out of the safe."

"Not a problem," the Candy Man offered. "I need to go and see my boy to pick up some more anyway. Y'all can ride with me." So the two officers got into the Candy Man's car and rode with him to secure the drugs. After the pickup, the officers started giving Candy Man directions to their office.

After a half-dozen lefts and rights, the three arrived in front of their "office."

"Well, here we are, Candy Man." The officers smiled.

"This ain't no office building, man. This is the police station."

"That's right," they assured him. "We're cops."

"Aw, man . . . you guys are the law?"

"'Fraid so," the officers answered. "And you're under arrest for sale of a controlled substance."

"Damn." The Candy Man just hung his head and sighed. "And I was beginning to like you guys."

It's like your mother always told you. It doesn't pay to talk to strangers.

It's the Law

In Sweden, it's illegal to drive on the highway if you have the flu—because reaction time of people with the flu tested below those with alcohol in their systems.

Here, we have convictions for D.U.I.—"Driving under the Influence."

Are sickly Swedes in danger of being charged with D.U.W.—"Driving Under the Weather"?

He Can Hide, but He Can't Run

20

Terry Jarnigan was a troublemaker. He was always having brushes with the law, and he was especially well known for starting fights and somehow managing to get away just before the police arrived.

One Friday night Terry tried to pick up another man's wife in a local tavern in a Midwest town, and a fight ensued. Soon the whole place was involved in an old-fashioned barroom brawl, with chairs and glasses being thrown and broken amidst a frenzied free-for-all.

Then someone yelled "Cops!" The crowd broke for the door, and Jarnigan was one of the first ones out. But the squad car pulled in, lights flashing, just as he was making his way across the parking lot. With no time to think and few places to run, Jarnigan opened the door of a brown Pontiac Bonneville and stretched out along the back floorboard.

In a matter of minutes, more officers and squad cars had pulled into the parking lot. Jarnigan would have to sit tight for a while. He just lay there in the back of the Pontiac, watching the shadows of the flashing lights and listening to the voices outside. He couldn't hear everything that was said as the police began arresting the people involved in the donnybrook. But he did hear his own name over and over as bar patrons explained the origins of the fight.

Then Terry Jarnigan heard voices coming closer to his hiding place.

"It's not fair to arrest me!" a man was protesting in a shrill voice. "I didn't start the fight. Some jerk was hitting on my wife, and she didn't like it. Well, I didn't like it either, so I just . . . "

"Yes, sir," another voice answered calmly. "We'll get all of that sorted out down at the police station. But we don't have any more room in the cruisers, so you'll have to follow me downtown in your own vehicle."

"He's the one you ought to be arresting . . . " The man was still muttering as he swung open the door of his brown Pontiac Bonneville. Terry Jarnigan blinked as the dome light came on, and the car's owner jumped back and yelled.

"Hey! Here he is—here's the punk that started the whole thing! You just wait till I get my . . . "

The officer stopped the furious husband just before he took hold of the cowering troublemaker. Jarnigan was duly booked for inciting a riot and for committing illegal trespass in entering the man's car. And then he was thrown into the same holding tank with the people he had provoked into fighting in the bar only an hour earlier, including the enraged husband of the woman he had flirted with.

They were all very glad to see him.

Lovin' in Fifteen Minutes

Is speeding a crime of passion? Officer Rusty Martin remembers a time when the label could have applied.

"I was a rookie stationed in a little town called Duncan, Mississippi," Martin says. "Now, nothing much ever happened in Duncan. The nights were even quieter than the days, and I was working the 6:00 P.M. to 3:00 A.M. shift. So I was always looking for ways to liven up those long hours."

One night Martin, who lived about thirty miles on the other end of the county, was headed home down the dark, quiet country lanes. He was in a hurry to get home and had already exceeded the speed limit when he noticed headlights in the distance behind him, closing in fast. Martin didn't have radar at that time, so he tried to pace the car behind him.

"I clicked it up to about eighty in order to get an indication of how fast he was going. Sure enough, he caught up with me easily. Then he saw the bar lights on my squad car and slammed on his brakes."

The late-night speedster climbed out of his car and read the officer's badge. "Please Officer Martin!" he begged. "You can't write me a ticket. I can't afford it—I just can't afford the ticket. Please just let me off with a warning."

It was very late. Martin was bored and just a little punchy, so he decided to have some fun. "I'll tell you what I'll do," he said. "If you can give me an excuse I haven't heard before, I won't write you this ticket."

The speedster didn't hesitate. "I left home about five o'clock this afternoon, and I told my wife, 'Honey, I won't be gone long.' Well, I got down to Mount Bayou, and we got to gambling, and I lost most of my money, so I had to stay until I could win some of it back."

Martin just nodded, pen in hand.

"Then my wife called," the speeder continued. "She said, 'There's going to be a whole lot of lovin' going on in this house in fifteen minutes, and if you want to be in on it, you had better be here.' That was fourteen minutes ago, and I'm trying my best to get there."

"The man wasn't joking," Martin remembers. "And I had to admit I never heard that one before. I let him go. What happened after that is anybody's guess."

Look Out! He's Got a Turtle and He Knows How to Use It!

It was a classic case of love gone wrong in Indiana. Boy meets girl. Boy falls in love. Girl doesn't.

In this case, she really did try to let him down easy, but he was distraught. He was fuming as he barreled out of her kitchen door and into the night.

The brokenhearted Romeo staggered through the fields in the throes of lover's angst. Then he saw his weapon, seized it, and started back to his girlfriend's house.

In a rage, Romeo returned and chased his ex-girlfriend around the kitchen with a large snapping turtle. He was much faster than Juliet and he easily caught her in the small kitchen, but he couldn't get the turtle to bite her. Finally, Juliet managed to call the police. The officers

He was much faster than Juliet and he easily caught her in the small kitchen, but he couldn't get the turtle to bite her.

arrived, disarmed (deturtled?) the irate lover, and arrested him for assault with a reptile.

The incident marked the definite end of one relationship, but the beginning of another. Juliet thought the big turtle was cute, and she was ever so grateful that he hadn't bitten her. The girl and the turtle are still together and living happily in Pennsylvania, according to the policeman who retold the story.

Luck of the Draw

With Oregon State Lottery ticket in hand, Alice Krumm stood staring at the winning numbers posted on the cash register. So close . . . but not quite. The ticket she had just bought was only one digit away from the twenty-dollar winning number. For once in her life, Alice wanted to be a winner instead of a near-miss.

Alice struggled with her greed for a long minute before finally giving in. Creeping around behind the baked beans and canned goods, she altered her lottery ticket with a ballpoint pen to win the twenty dollars, then returned to the counter to collect her ill-gotten prize.

But she should have worked a little harder on her forgery. The clerk spotted it immediately and called the police. The dishonest lottery player was arrested on the spot and charged with fraud.

Then the arresting officer made an interesting discovery. He found the real number under her bad forgery. His revelation made her feel even dumber.

Had she looked farther up the chart of winning numbers, she would have discovered that her original ticket number had also been a winner—for five thousand dollars!

Pulling the Rug Out

In Peoria, Illinois, police were called to the scene of a home burglary. The perplexed homeowners reported that the house had indeed been burglarized, but that none of the normal things were missing. The television and VCR were still there, although each had been moved a little. A stereo system, jewelry, and even some cash all could be accounted for. It turned out that only one major item was missing—but it was a significant one. An entire houseful of new wall-to-wall carpet had been taken up and stolen.

The officers on the scene were as perplexed as the burglary victims. They really had no idea how to track a hot carpet. Scratching their heads, they headed outside into the newly fallen snow to look around.

But wait! What's this? In the yard, footprints showed on either side of a long, scraped trail leading out toward a nearby field. Either the carpet had been dragged in that direction, or a brontosaurus had just strolled by.

The officers followed the trail across the yard, through the field, and into another yard, where the trail ended at a neighbor's front door.

When the police entered the small home behind a larger main house, they found not a brontosaurus, but the stolen carpet on the floor—recut and laid to fit its new home. The young man who lived there insisted that he had purchased the rug, but the police showed him his own trail from the "carpet store." He was arrested and charged with the crime.

Don't Try It Again, Sam

25

In Thibodaux, Louisiana, a blundering, wannabe robber with speech difficulties just couldn't win for losing. Sam Lincoln entered Bob's Cafe and, speaking in his thick, backwoods Cajun accent, ordered the waitress to "give me all the money."

Unfortunately, she couldn't understand a word he said. To her it sounded like he was ordering "a sieve with all the honey."

In desperation, Sam turned to a patron and told him to hand over all *his* money. The diner could have sworn that Sam said to "live a big pile of bunny."

When the patron couldn't understand him either, Sam got so frustrated that he pulled out his gun. Now they would hear the unmistakable voice of his thirty-eight.

Sam pulled the trigger.

Click.

The gun wouldn't fire.

Now Sam grabbed the cash register and began to run. But he didn't get far—only about three feet. The register was still firmly plugged into the wall, and he quickly ran out of cord.

The register was jerked out of Sam's hands, and he fell. Humiliated and frustrated, he ran out of Bob's Cafe empty-handed. Waitresses and patrons breathed a sigh of relief. Someone hefted the register back up to its place on the counter.

But five minutes later, Sam was back. This time, he made sure he unplugged the register before making off with it. Sam was ecstatic—for about three feet. A bystander who had witnessed the whole comedy of errors knocked Sam down and made a citizen's arrest.

Bound for the Cooler

26

One bright spring morning in Lafayette, Louisiana, Louis Albright had the bright idea of robbing a branch of a local bank. Louis had an even more brilliant idea for a low-cost, low-fat, completely disposable disguise. He would cover his entire head with whipped cream.

A few trial runs indicated his idea would work beautifully. The foamy "mask" sprayed on quickly and was easily wiped off. It completely covered any distinguishing marks, even his hair color. And it tasted wonderful, to boot.

Congratulating himself on his innovative idea, the human hot-fudge sundae walked into the bank and approached the teller. Unfortunately, the employees' response to his delicious disguise was just the opposite of what he wanted. The giggles were discreet at first, but when he said, "Put all your money in the sack," the giggles dissolved into open laughter.

By this time the whipped cream was getting warm and beginning to slide. And the teller had long ago punched the silent alarm. Before you could say "banana split," the police arrived. The rapidly melting bank robber was quickly arrested and refrigerated downtown.

By this time the whipped cream was getting warm and beginning to slide. And the teller had long ago punched the silent alarm.

Two-Bit Thief

Rhode Island police were sure they had the right man when the suspect charged with a string of vending-machine robberies paid his four-hundred-dollar bail entirely in quarters.

A Really Big Bust

At first, the customs officer thought the drug-sniffing dog was barking up the wrong tree. Or, rather, sniffing up the wrong tourist.

As the 475-pound man waddled through customs, the dog began to pay him close attention, sniffing suspiciously at the man's huge stomach. Annoyed, the man told the dog to "shoo." No luck.

The customs officer was a bit reluctant to approach the man, since he really didn't fit the profile of a smuggler, and his personal effects had already been examined. But the dog was relentless. Over and over it pointed its nose toward the tourist and kept sniffing and whining and sniffing. It was almost as though the dog itself was puzzled.

The officer finally conceded that something was awry.

"I'm sorry, sir," he told the rotund tourist. "I'm afraid you're going to have to accompany me to a dressing room for a strip search."

It was a task that neither man was looking forward to. But it had to be done.

Once inside the room, the tourist was ordered to disrobe, and a complete body search was initiated. It was then that a plastic bag containing eleven ounces of a white powdery substance was discovered—discreetly hidden amid the many folds of the man's tremendous stomach!

The substance proved to be cocaine.

The drug dog was vindicated.

Bare Truth

In a small town in Texas late on a Saturday afternoon, a small mom-and-pop store was robbed by a lone gunman. The prime suspect was quickly spotted. In fact, everybody in town spotted him. They didn't even need a detailed description. The fleeing felon was running down the street completely naked.

But Ted Jowers had a great alibi ready for the police officers who stopped him. "I like to get in touch with nature when I jog," he told them.

Somehow, though, Ted didn't seem like the nature type—or the jogging type, for that matter. The officers brought him in.

Ted finally broke down and confessed to the robbery. Then he explained to the police that he had stripped down to streak away after the robbery because he thought his clothes would make him more identifiable.

Ah, the ironic naked truth of the dumb criminal plan.

30 Love Thy Neighbor

The weary, disheveled woman tossed and turned in her bed. It was two in the morning, and the trucks at the nearby warehouse were grinding their gears, braking loudly, and making that maddening "Beep! Beep! Beep!" sound that a postal truck makes when in reverse gear.

What is so important that you have to truck it in the middle of the night? she wondered.

Finally, the unwilling insomniac could stand no more. She called the police and complained about the noise.

A quick check downtown revealed that the warehouse was leased to a toy import company. That set the officers to wondering. Christmas was still many months away. Why would a toy company be working round the clock to ship Chinese dolls and robots that spew smoke?

Ten minutes later, the two officers who had been sent to follow up on the disturbing-the-peace complaint pulled their cruiser up behind the working docks. When they stepped out of their vehicle, the men on the loading dock scattered and disappeared into the night.

The officers figured they must have a burglary in progress and called for backup. Three of the men were quickly apprehended in the neighborhood, but they turned out to be the rightful occupants of the warehouse.

So why had they fled?

Well, they weren't burglars, but they were guilty of a bit more than disturbing the peace. The police searched the warehouse and ended up seizing twenty-two tons of cocaine, with a street value of more than six billion dollars.

It was the biggest drug raid in U.S. history, and it carries a lesson for all would-be dumb criminals: If you're going to mess with Uncle Sam, make sure you don't wake up the neighbors!

DUMB CRIMINAL QUIZ NO. 007

How well do you know the dumb criminal mind?

An officer fired at a bearded burglary suspect. The fleeing felon was unhurt, but the bullet tore a hole in the man's shirt as it flapped in the breeze. The criminal escaped. Immediately afterward, did he . . .

- (a) sew his shirt while he watched television?
- (b) shave his beard and go right down to the police station?
- (c) use his shirt as a hand puppet to entertain children?
- (d) try and take his shirt back for a refund?

If your answer was (b), you are correct. In Atlanta, a burglar was fired at by officers, escaped unhurt, and returned to his own home. When he got home, he quickly shaved his beard to fool the police and then went right to the police station to report that his car had been stolen. He was arrested on the spot.

Why? First, in his haste, he had cut himself shaving, so his face was a bloody mess. Oh, and he also forgot to change the shirt that had the bullet hole in it.

Five Will Get You Ten or Twenty-Five

With a long sigh, Janice Patterson finished writing her check on her account and received the five-dollar bill from the bank teller. She actually needed more, but her balance was far too low at the moment. She wouldn't get her next paycheck for two more days. Until then, she would just have to get by on those five dollars.

Janice got into her car, swung the door shut, and put the key in the ignition. Just as she was starting the engine, a man jumped in the front seat beside her and pointed a gun right at her face. "Give me all your money—right now!" he demanded in a harsh voice.

Reluctantly, but obediently, Janice turned over her five-dollar bill.

"It's all I have," she explained.

"You're kidding!" The bad guy put the gun down. Incredulous, he searched her purse and the glove compartment before he finally realized she was telling the truth.

"Damn—wouldn't you know it! All those people

comin' out of the bank, and I have to pick the one that don't got no money!"

All Janice could do was shrug. But now her would-be robber decided to take a different approach. "Write me a check!" he ordered.

But Janice had to shrug again. She had just written the last of the checks in her checkbook.

Obviously, this was not going well at all for our criminal.

"I gotta think!" he mused, then ordered her to drive around the block. Janice obeyed.

They had just turned the corner when another problem apparently occurred to the worried criminal. His victim had seen what he looked like and presumably could relay his description to the police.

"Don't look at me," he warned. "You keep looking at the floor, hear me?"

"That would be difficult," she told the crook. "I'm driving, remember?"

"Well, you just look straight ahead. Don't look at me."

She didn't.

Momentarily frustrated, the bandit then remembered that banks keep counter checks available for customer use. He directed his victim to drive back to the bank.

They went inside to one of the desks, where he directed her to write a check for eighty-five dollars. She didn't bother to tell him she didn't have that much in the account. But she did try to communicate with the teller. As the bandit fidgeted and glanced around, Janice gestured, mimed, made faces, and even pointed at the man, but her dramatics had no effect on the teller.

Resigning herself to the victim's role, the woman handed the check to the bandit, but in her nervousness she neglected to sign it.

The teller, finally tipped of by the omission of the signature, slipped back to the manager's office, where a call was made to police. The robber was arrested, convicted, and sentenced to ten years in jail.

Janice Patterson barely escaped punishment herself.

"It's a good thing you didn't sign it," the teller pointed out to her. "The check would have bounced, and we would have had to charge you a twenty-five-dollar processing fee."

32 Big Mac Attackers

Retired Officer David Hunter of the Knox County (Tennessee) Sheriff's Department tells this story of two very hungry holdup men:

After an evening of partying and smoking dope, the two very high potheads decided they would kill two birds with one stone. They were broke, and they had the "munchies," so they agreed that the best thing to do would be to rob a hamburger joint. Armed with loaded shotguns, they burst through the door of the first place they came upon.

"Give us all the money," the dim-bulb duo demanded, "and a dozen hamburgers with everything—to go!"

"I'll get you the money, man," one frightened employee replied, "but the grill's already been shut down. It'll take about ten minutes to reheat."

"Do it," came the gunman's reply. "We'll wait!"

Meanwhile, a passing motorist noticed that the two

men sitting in the burger shack were holding shotguns. Suspicious indeed. The motorist phoned police.

"Here's your food," the shaking worker said.

The burger bandits grabbed the greasy sack and hit the door just as the sound of police sirens and squealing tires filled the night air. In their haste, they left the stolen money sitting on the table.

Panicked, the two robbers ran across a highway, slid down an embankment, and tried to hide under a bridge, which is where the K-9 unit found them. The hamburger heist was over.

"What really pisses me off," one man said to the other as they were being led away in handcuffs, "is that those damn dogs ate all our burgers. I didn't even get one bite!"

The officer responded, "You ought to be glad those are the only buns the dog bit."

33 In the Mood

Trooper Robert Bell shared this story of true romance at a very tender age in the Southeast:

Bell was headed out to the interstate highway through a small town when he noticed a classic car whipping by at a high rate of speed. It was a '64 Buick in mint condition. Radar revealed the vehicle was traveling at fifty miles per hour—*over* the speed limit.

When Bell closed in on the Buick, the speeder acted as if he might force a chase, but then he abruptly pulled over. Bell approached the idling Buick carefully. When he got to the window, he saw that the driver was an elderly man who appeared to be quite agitated.

"Sir," the trooper said, "were you aware that you were doing eighty-five in a thirty-five-mile-per-hour zone?"

"Of course I know how fast I'm going," the driver snapped. "It's an emergency!"

Concerned, the officer asked, "Is it a medical emergency, sir? I can get you to a hospital."

The driver's face reddened. "No, I have to go now. It's an emergency!"

"What's the emergency, sir? Maybe I can help you."

The old gentleman just looked angrier than ever. "I can't tell you. You'll laugh at me."

Bell tried to reassure him. "I won't laugh at you, sir. But if you don't tell me what the emergency is, I'll have to write you a ticket."

The senior speedster finally relented. "You promise not to laugh—man to man?" He was very serious.

"No, sir," Bell said. "I promise."

"Well, son, I'm eighty-two years old, and I haven't had an erec-uh . . . well, I haven't been 'in the mood for love' for more than two years now. Well, I have an—uh, I'm in the mood right now, and I'm on my way to my girl-friend's house!"

Bell was stunned, but only for a moment. "I had never heard that excuse for speeding before and—man to man—well, I had to empathize just a little. So I gave him a police escort."

There's One Born Every Minute

Circus man P. T. Barnum is famous for saying that there's a sucker born every minute. Retired captain Don Parker of the Escambia County Sheriff's Department in Pensacola, Florida, reports an unusual incident that proves Mr. Barnum's point:

A resident of a quiet neighborhood was walking his dog in the woods one evening when the animal sniffed out a woman's purse. The man unzipped the purse to look for identification. Instead of a wallet, a comb, or a lipstick, he found several curious packages, about the size of small bricks, wrapped in plastic and sealed with duct tape. Suspicious, he called the cops.

A patrolling deputy soon arrived and took the purse and its contents back to the station. As suspected, the packages contained drugs—pure cocaine with an estimated street value of two hundred thousand dollars.

The narcotics division immediately set up surveillance at the site where the purse had been found, hoping that someone would try to retrieve the drugs. But there was no activity, even though the officers stayed until well after midnight. Finally, as they were about to give up, one of them had a brilliant idea.

"Give me a piece of paper," he whispered to his partner. Then he wrote, "I found your purse and the contents. Call me. Large reward expected." He listed one of the confidential phone numbers that bypassed the department's switchboard and rang directly in the narcotics office.

The narcotics officer quickly taped the note to a stick and placed it where the purse had been. Then he and his partner went home.

The narcotics officers' fellow workers were highly amused the next morning when they learned about the note. For the rest of the day, the two were teased unmercifully. But the jokes stopped abruptly when they got a call around three in the afternoon.

A female cop answered the phone and set the trap. She demanded ten thousand dollars in cash for the safe return of the purse and its contents. At first the person on the other end of the line balked, but she made it clear he would have to pay up if he wanted the dope back. Finally, he agreed.

The drop was set for a phone booth outside the local mall. Undercover deputies took up positions in the parking lot around the booth.

The male and female narcotics officers stood by the phone booth, the female cop holding the purse. Soon a car with three occupants pulled up.

One suspect got out of the car and handed the narcotics officers a shopping bag that was bulging with cash. The female undercover officer gave the suspect the purse, and the man turned to go back to his car. That's when the cops got the drop on the suspects.

When both cops drew their weapons, the suspect started to go for his own, but thought better of it. Seeing that his friend was in trouble, the driver of the car did what had to be done—he prepared to save his own tail. Before he could get the car in gear, however, he found himself staring down the gun barrels of about a dozen policemen.

The final score was six pounds of cocaine, ten thousand dollars in cash, three suspects arrested, one car confiscated, and a nice leather purse. And the bust might never have been made if that one narcotics officer hadn't posted the sign.

It just goes to show: There *is* a sucker born every minute. And it always pays to advertise.

The Sad Saga of Bad Luck Brown

35

Don Parker of Pensacola also has a string of tales to tell about a dumb criminal who richly earned his nickname of Bad Luck Brown.

"We called him that because this guy had atrocious luck," Parker remembers. "Plus he wasn't all that bright. He was a small-time crook who spent more time in jail than he did out.

"I think the first time I met Bad Luck was in 1978 when I rolled in on a robbery call at a church on Sunday morning during the sermon. Bad Luck had robbed the collection plate. He made good on his escape and got away clean with all the cash, but he dropped his wallet. All we had to do was check his driver's license, then go by his house and pick him up."

But the dumbest crime Bad Luck Brown ever committed was one of his unluckiest, too.

There had been a string of motel robberies in the Pensacola area, and the police had received a tip on where the motel thieves were going to hit next. They always hit the motels around midnight, and the cops planned to be ready for them. Officers were stationed in the motel office and in parked cars around the parking lot. Parker was in the woods across the street with three other officers.

Just past midnight, an old, beat-up station wagon slowly passed the motel. It rattled up the road, turned around, and came back. The vehicle didn't fit the description of the motel robbers, and there was only one person in the car. But the motel thieves might have changed cars, or they might have just been casing the place. All the hidden officers watched it carefully.

The car turned around and came back for a third pass. Don Parker called his sergeant across the street on his walkie-talkie. "You think this might be our guys?"

"Nah, but he sure is interested in something."

The car stopped, a door opened, the driver leaned out and looked around cautiously. The sergeant wasn't taking any chances.

"All units stand by. We've got some activity out here, but I don't know what's going on."

Everybody watched as the mystery man stepped from the car.

"He's on the ground." The man walked around his vehicle and into the light of a street lamp. "He's on the

But Bad Luck Brown's luck held true. Just as he was about to disappear, he tripped over one of the officers and sprained his ankle.

street side of his car now. Okay, I can see him now . . . oh, no!'

Parker didn't like the tone of Sarge's voice. "What? What?"

Sarge radioed back, "It's Bad Luck Brown."

The man eased over to the patch of grass in front of the motel and finally stopped next to a lawn mower that someone had carelessly left out.

Sarge was almost laughing. "I don't believe it. He's stealing the lawn mower!"

Quickly and silently, Bad Luck Brown rolled the lawn mower to his station wagon, dropped the tailgate, and loaded the mower into his car.

"Move in." Sarge gave the command with a bit of resigned frustration in his voice.

The two unmarked cars in the parking lot pulled up to block the station wagon just as Bad Luck started it up. The officers hopped out with drawn guns and called him to freeze. Instead, Bad Luck jumped out and made a run for it. He dashed across the street into the woods—right where Parker was hiding.

"We almost scared him to death when we jumped out. But he was determined to get away this time, so he bolted to the left into the dense undergrowth. Now, a foot chase at night in the woods is the worst. You're running into trees and falling down into gullies. So I decided to try to scare him into stopping.

"'Halt, or I'll shoot!' I fired my gun into the ground. Unfortunately, this didn't have the effect I had hoped for. All the officers hit the ground, but Bad Luck just sped up. It looked like he was going to get away clean."

But Bad Luck Brown's luck held true. Just as he was about to disappear, he tripped over one of the officers and sprained his ankle.

"We never did see the motel thieves that night," Parker says. "But once again, it was our privilege to book Bad Luck Brown. He never ceased to amaze us."

Another Run of Bad Luck Brown

Yet another story about the notorious Bad Luck Brown from Pensacola, Florida, involves a time when this dumb criminal's bad luck *almost* changed.

One sunny afternoon Bad Luck Brown entered a busy liquor store with the intent of robbing it. Once he got into the store, however, there were too many people around for a real stickup, so he switched to Plan B. Fishing in his pocket for a piece of paper, Bad Luck scrawled a note to the cashier demanding money.

The cashier read the note and quickly handed over all the money in the drawer. In a flash, Bad Luck was out the door and gone. He seemed to have pulled off his robbery with flawless precision.

Except for one thing.

When the police arrived on the scene, they found the holdup note used in the robbery. When they turned it over, they knew exactly who to go after and where to find him.

Bad Luck Brown had written the note on the back of a letter he had received from his probation officer—complete with his name and address. When police tracked him down at home, they were able to inform him that his streak of bad luck was still intact.

This explosion, they believed, would pour millions of cubic feet of water onto the helpless city, transforming Nashville into a sort of country-and-western Atlantis.

A Dam Dumb Idea

In the great state of Tennessee three fools came up with a plan to make themselves rich. They were going to knock off the entire city of Nashville.

Our schemers needed a few supplies. Dynamite, for instance—lots of dynamite. Their warped plan was to blow up Percy Priest Dam approximately ten miles east of the city. This explosion, they believed, would pour millions of cubic feet of water onto the helpless city, transforming Nashville into a sort of country-and-western Atlantis. Then they would don their scuba gear, swim through the submerged city, and steal all the Rolexes, diamond rings, and money they could carry.

Bizarre, yes, but that was the plan. Our three aquatic airheads bought some dynamite, carried it to the dam, and succeeded in setting it off. The small explosion did little serious damage. The scheme wasn't even discovered until a short time later, when the explosive conspirators were captured and arrested.

Arrest Record

The record for being arrested belongs to Tommy Johns of Brisbane, Australia. By 1985, Tommy had been arrested for drunkenness two thousand times, according to Brisbane police. His total number of arrests for public drunkenness at the time of his death in 1988 was "nearly three thousand."

Legend has it that when Tommy was cremated, it took three weeks to put out the fire.

It's the Law

In the 1980s, New York's nonviolent offenders were allowed to choose sidewalk sweeping or trash collecting instead of jail time.

Of the first one hundred arrested, ninety-seven chose jail time!

They all knew that jail was safer than the sidewalks of New York City—probably cleaner, too.

The Light at the End of the Tennie

Just outside Lawrence, Kansas, police were called to an all-night market that had just been robbed. A male Caucasian had brandished a weapon and demanded money from a store employee. After stuffing the money into his pants pocket, he fled down the street.

Units in the area responded quickly to the alarm. Within moments, two officers on patrol had spotted a man running behind some houses in a nearby neighborhood. Certain that they had the right man, they gave chase on foot.

But the suspect wasn't really worried. It was dark, he was a very fast runner, and he knew the neighborhood like the back of his hand. He was sure he would have no trouble eluding the cops.

It didn't take long for the fleet-footed suspect to leave the first pair of officers behind, but he was surprised when more officers quickly joined in the chase. Each time the thief would elude one officer, he would be

The pursuing officers had just followed the lights.

spotted by another. The crook couldn't understand it; he was using his best moves.

At last there were too many officers on the scene who apparently could see quite well in the dark. Our suspect looked frustrated and surprised when he was finally captured.

But he was even more surprised and frustrated once the police told him how they knew where he was all the time. He really hadn't been hard to follow at all, thanks to advanced technology.

The pursuing officers had just followed the lights. Not the infrared lights used for night vision, but the red lights on the heels of the suspect's high-tech tennis shoes—the ones that blinked on and off every time his feet hit the ground.

Possession Is Nine-Tenths of the Law

In Edina, Minnesota, two would-be robbers hit on a foolproof getaway plan—or so they thought. Rather than using one of their own vehicles, which would be traced directly back to their home, they decided to steal a pickup truck right before they robbed the bank.

Two blocks from the bank, they found a really nice pickup easy to hot wire. They then parked their stolen pickup outside the Norton Bank while they went inside to rob it.

So far, so good. But those bandits hadn't figured on the determination of the pickup's owner, who had spotted them driving away and sprinted after them.

The two clever thieves got a substantial haul of money from the bank and then ran outside to find their stolen truck had been, well . . . stolen. The original owner had reclaimed it while they were busy at the bank. Panicked, the robbers attempted their getaway on foot, but they failed. The next pickup in this story was by the police.

The hapless robber finally made it to his truck with a fistful of greenbacks, only to have his car key break off in the door. As if that wasn't bad enough, he shot himself in the foot with his revolver while struggling to open the locked door.

All Thumbs

There are some days when nothing seems to go right—and this is truer of dumb criminals than it is of most of us.

Near Cleveland, Ohio, a lone gunman entered a cafe, pointed a gun at the waitress, and announced, "This is a robbery!" The waitress filled a paper bag with money as instructed, and the gunman escaped with the cash. But as the man ran across the parking lot the bag tore open, spilling bills and coins across the asphalt.

The hapless robber finally made it to his truck with a fistful of greenbacks, only to have his car key break off in the door. As if that wasn't bad enough, he shot himself in the foot with his revolver while struggling to open the locked door.

A few minutes later, he hobbled into a hospital emergency room. The police were notified and the footloose, clumsy, unlucky bandit was arrested.

What's the Number for 911?

Dumb criminals usually do their best to avoid arrest, but there are exceptions even to that rule. Charlie Hackett, chief of police in Kokomo, Indiana, remembers a criminal who decided the police were by far the lesser of the evils confronting him.

"There was a guy in town we'd had some problems with," Hackett recalls. "He was only about eighteen or nineteen years old, but he'd been arrested several times as a juvenile and was generally a troublemaker. And now he was wanted on a warrant for a burglary. So I was surprised when he called me on the phone at the station."

At the time, Hackett was a lieutenant working the detective division. His desk was in a large, busy room, and the room was so noisy he could hardly hear anything.

Hackett answered the phone and barely heard someone whispering, "Hello? Hello? Is this Lieutenant Hackett?"

The lieutenant put a hand over his other ear and shouted into the phone. "Could you speak up a little bit?"

"This is Joe Miller," whispered the voice on the other end.

"Joe, why are you being so quiet?" Lieutenant Hackett asked. Then he added, "We have a warrant for your arrest, you know."

"I know," Joe answered. "That's why I'm calling you . . . to turn myself in."

Over the phone, in the background, Hackett could hear a strange boom, boom, boom—like someone pounding on a door.

"C'mon Joe," he repeated, "speak up. I can't hear you."

"I can't talk very loud. I just wanted to turn myself in—come get me right away."

It turned out that an angry father and his son had caught Joe messing around with the man's daughter. Now they had Joe cornered in a room. One was at the front door, and one was at the back door. Turning himself in was just Joe's way of asking for police protection.

He figured—no doubt correctly—that almost any amount of jail time would be less painful than five minutes alone with that woman's father.

Backseat Driver

When police pull over a driver, they're always ready to hear the "big story." Sergeant Doug Baldwin of the Pensacola (Florida) Police Department remembers a time when a van was swerving and weaving across the center line. When the officer approached the van, now stopped, he noticed that the driver had moved over to the passenger's seat.

The officer shined his flashlight across the front seat to the man who had suddenly become the passenger in a driverless van. The officer asked for the man's driver's license and registration.

"I wasn't driving," the man claimed and pointed to the backseat. "The guy in the back was."

The officer shined his flashlight in back and got a good look at the perpetrator—a huge teddy bear.

It didn't take the officer long to assess the situation. One of the van's occupants was stuffed. The other was obviously loaded.

Door-to-Door Crime Buster

An officer in Savannah developed a bold but simple approach to drug busts. This uniformed patrolman would walk up to a known drug house or party and knock on the door. The occupant would answer the door with almost the same greeting every time. In fact, the similarity of the incidents was astounding. Each person reacted in almost the same manner every time the officer tried this very direct approach to crime busting. It went something like this:

Dumb Criminal opens door. "Uh . . . hello, officer. Is the music too loud? Did someone complain?"

"Nah, I just wanted to buy a bag of dope."

"Huh?"

"Do you have a bag of dope I can buy?"

"Well . . . but you're a cop."

"So? Can't I buy a bag of dope?"

"But . . . "

"Hey, I'm cool, okay?"

"Cool. Wait right here."

A minute later, the dumb (and about-to-be arrested) criminal would be selling the uniformed officer a bag of dope.

The bold officer made so many arrests this way that he was promoted to detective in record time. Almost all of his arrests were pleaded out without a trial because the criminals didn't want to admit in court they had sold drugs to a uniformed cop at their own apartment.

Drag Race

It was another routine day on patrol at a shopping mall. Officer Dusty Cutler had just grabbed a quick lunch and returned to her squad car when she saw a blond woman sprint out the mall entrance and into the parking lot.

"She was an attractive woman," Cutler remembers. "She wore a nice print dress, high heels . . . and she was very tall."

But why was she running? Seconds later Cutler got an answer when two men ran out the door and pursued the woman across the parking lot.

At first, Cutler thought the two men were harassing the woman. Then they got closer, and she heard them shouting, "Stop her! She robbed us!"

Cutler later learned that the woman had shoplifted women's clothing from a store in the mall and then assaulted one of the managers. The two men chasing her through the busy parking lot were the store's other manager and a salesclerk.

As the suspect ran in front of Cutler's car, she hiked up her dress in order to run faster, exposing a large pair of women's underwear. They were bulkier than normal, and Cutler could see a sleeve from a woman's blouse sticking out through the leg opening.

As the shoplifter sprinted away, the large baggy underwear stuffed with stolen merchandise slipped down over the suspect's thighs. At that point the officer noticed something extra that obviously didn't come from a store. The woman shoplifter, evidently, was not a woman.

By now the officer was having a difficult time calling in the report because she was laughing so hard. And the fleeing shoplifter was rapidly losing ground. With every step, the loaded underwear slipped farther down the suspect's legs. Finally, they fell to the ground and sent their wearer sprawling.

Still trying to make a graceful getaway, the fugitive scrambled back up, kicked off both the offending underwear and the high heels, and ran faster. But by this time Cutler had pulled the patrol car into the suspect's path, and the fleeing criminal slammed across the hood of the car. She/he was arrested and charged with shoplifting.

Cutler still speaks of that shoplifter-in-drag as the strangest criminal she ever—literally—ran into.

The woman had shoplifted women's clothing from a store in the mall and then assaulted one of the managers.

 **Bad Bribes**

A New York cop was working traffic one night when a muscular chap in a small car zipped right through a red light. When the officer pulled the vehicle over and made his approach, the driver immediately identified his occupation. The officer was interested, but not particularly impressed, to learn that the guilty motorist was a masseur. The officer was writing out the ticket when the masseur attempted to bribe the officer by offering him a massage.

He got the ticket anyway—perhaps because the whole experience just rubbed the officer the wrong way.

Type Ohhhhhhh!

When Charlie Beavers broke into a plasma center one Saturday night in Pensacola, Florida, he didn't get much —primarily because he didn't get too far.

Now, to a normal, rational mind, breaking into a plasma center might not make much sense. But to Charlie, it seemed like a good idea at the time. So after checking out the building, Charlie removed the top from an air vent on the roof and entered feet first. *Great*, he thought. *I'll just slide down this air vent, steal everything in sight, and make a clean getaway.*

His master plan was going flawlessly until the shaft did a nine-foot vertical drop, causing him to lose his grip. Charlie shot down the duct at a high rate of speed. The experience must have seemed like a ride at the fair— but the ride came to a sudden and painful stop.

Charlie's air shaft ended approximately three feet above a cross beam that separated two offices. And Charlie reached terminal velocity at about the same time he reached the cross beam. With a force hard enough to break through two ceilings (one leg on each side of the beam), he came to a crushing halt.

Charlie's legs were now in separate rooms. His arms were wedged tightly inside the shaft, straight up over his head. He was snugly straddling a cross beam.

Charlie spent a long weekend waiting for help. It arrived two days later, in the form of the police responding to a "breaking and entering" call. But then the police had to wait for the fire department to come and extricate Charlie from his predicament. As the luckless burglar was led hobbling away, Officer Pete Bell noticed that "part of his anatomy had swollen up to grapefruit size. And being from Florida, we know our grapefruits."

Beavers was arrested and charged with breaking and entering. Most officers on the scene agreed that Charlie had served his sentence long before the police ever arrived.

Oh, did we mention that it rained all weekend, right down the shaft and onto Charlie's face?

Sticky Situation

Metropolitan Nashville Police Officer Jeb Johnson gave *America's Dumbest Criminals* this scoop about an alarming crime:

While browsing at a chic clothier, nineteen-year-old Jonathan Parker decided that he needed three leather jackets in the worst way. The price was a little too steep, though, so Jonathan decided that he would take a "five-finger discount." That is, he was going to steal them.

Jonathan surveyed the premises and spotted every shoplifter's nightmare, a sensor alarm in front of the shop's exit. He knew the merchandise was tagged with magnetic strips, and if he tried to slip out with any tagged merchandise, the sensor would set off a deafening siren.

Undaunted, Jonathan grabbed some jackets that suited his taste and ducked into the nearest dressing room. Thoroughly searching the jackets, our shoplifter found all the magnetic strips and peeled them off. He found them inside sleeves and pockets, under collars and along the waistband. Jonathan was very proud of himself as he flicked the last of the strips onto the floor. He stuffed the jackets under his coat and boldly walked toward the front door.

A second later the loud, piercing scream of the alarm alerted the security guard, who quickly apprehended our thorough young thief. Jonathan was stunned. Hadn't he searched every inch of those jackets?

The security guard searched the stolen jackets, and he couldn't find any magnetic strips either. So why had the alarm gone off?

Then the guard looked a little deeper. He looked right into the sole—the sole of Jonathan's shoe, that is. And there he discovered four or five of the little magnetic strips, which Jonathan had thrown to the floor and then stepped on. The young man was arrested and charged with shoplifting.

Sticky fingers and sticky shoes—they'll get you every time.

Big Brother Is Watching You

Officer Pete Peterson, now an instructor at the Federal Law Enforcement Training Center in Brunswick, Georgia, was working patrol in a much burglarized Illinois neighborhood several years ago. There had been a robbery in the neighborhood and the perpetrator had been arrested, but the police were looking for a possible pickup car. Officer Peterson stopped a vehicle that fit the profile that had been circulated. He asked the driver for his license, and the man quickly complied.

Peterson glanced at the license, did a quiet double-take, then asked the driver to repeat the information on the license. The driver again cooperated. After several minutes of questioning, however, Peterson said, "I don't think you're Mark Peterson."

"What?" the driver protested. "No, that's me!"

"I don't think so," Peterson repeated.

"I don't know what you're getting at," the driver retorted

indignantly. "But I can't stand here all day. I've got an appointment."

For several more minutes he kept insisting the driver's license was his and that Pete was wasting his time.

Finally, Officer Peterson showed him his name badge. "You see, my name's Peterson. I've got a little brother named Mark, and this is his driver's license. My folks live at the address listed here. So I'm pretty sure that you stole this license!"

The driver just sank. "This has been the worst day for me," he sighed.

The day got even worse when he heard the jail door slam shut. He had three outstanding felony warrants for his arrest.

DUMB CRIMINAL QUIZ NO. 111

How well do you know the dumb criminal mind?

You're in Raritan, New Jersey, and you've just received a ticket. Now, let's play the matching game. Match the offense with the penalty.

OFFENSE	FINE
a) Littering	$500.00
b) D.U.I.	$250.00
c) Cursing in Public	$25.00
d) Public Display of Affection	Not an Offense

Answers: (a) $25.00 (b) $250.00 (c) $500.00 (d) usually not an offense—depending, we suppose, on how affectionate you get!

Going My Way?

It seems that some people go out of their way to get into trouble. That's more or less what happened the night that Nashville Police Officer Floyd A. Hyde unexpectedly became involved in a high-speed chase.

"I was en route to a personal-injury accident in West Nashville, and to get there I had to enter Interstate 40 from I-440. As I merged, blue lights and sirens going, I fell in behind a gold Pontiac Firebird that suddenly seemed to sprout wings and take off down the interstate. The driver apparently panicked at the sight of me. He accelerated to more than a hundred miles per hour and began passing cars on the shoulder. It was obvious that he thought I was after him and was making a run for it."

But Hyde couldn't give chase, despite the driver's reckless behavior. Injured people always take priority over traffic offenders, so the officer had to stay en route to the accident. But he did try to keep the Firebird in sight as he drove, hoping another nearby unit would be able to

"I saw fire billowing out from underneath that car, with blue smoke and oil going everywhere. He'd blown his engine. Now he had to stop."

step in and stop the speeding vehicle. As it turned out, keeping the Pontiac in sight was not that difficult. Every turn the Pontiac made was the very turn the officer needed to get to the accident scene.

Hyde followed the Pontiac all the way to his destination. At that point he found another unit had already arrived at the accident scene. His help wasn't needed. Now he was free to try to stop the nut in the Firebird, who by this time had developed something new to panic about.

"Just about the time my priorities changed," Hyde says, "I saw fire billowing out from underneath that car, with blue smoke and oil going everywhere. He'd blown his engine. Now he had to stop.

"After I arrested him, I asked him why he was running. He told me he had a suspended driver's license. When I told him that I hadn't been after him in the first place, that I would have simply gone around him if he hadn't taken off like that, *and* that I wouldn't have caught him if he hadn't made every turn I needed to make—well, he got pretty upset."

That incident cost the driver of the Firebird plenty—a thousand dollars for the new engine plus the expense of having his car towed—not to mention the charges for driving with a suspended license, attempting to elude, and reckless driving.

Asleep at the Wheel

Officer Lynn Flanders of the Escambia County Sheriff's Department in Pensacola, Florida, was dispatched to a convenience store where a man was exposing himself. Another female officer quickly joined her as backup. They arrived to find the flasher still on the scene—but sound asleep!

"The flasher was seated in his car in front of the store, totally naked, and snoring up a storm. So we knocked on the window and woke him up."

Flanders then explained to the snoozing streaker that he was under arrest for indecent exposure.

The sleepy-eyed criminal didn't seem all that perturbed, but he did have one request of his arresting officers: "Can I put my clothes on?"

The officers glanced around the car. The only clothes visible in the car were a pair of scuffed shoes and a wad of dirty socks lying on the passenger-side floorboard.

"Well, sir," Flanders told him, "you can put your shoes on if you want to, but I honestly don't think it'll make much difference!"

"Oh, no, Officer," the naked man explained earnestly. "My clothes are here. They're just stuck between the seats here."

Of course. Isn't that where we all keep our clothes when we sleep naked at the roadside convenience store?

Always willing to serve the public, the two officers helped the suspect retrieve his clothes and waited for him to dress before escorting the fully clothed and wide-awake flasher to his new temporary home in a holding cell.

I Can't Believe It

53

Once when Officer Donna McCown was working narcotics in a large southwestern city, her department head assigned her to secure two hundred dollars' worth of crack cocaine from a known drug dealer who had been arrested several times.

McCown had some concerns about the assignment because, as she remembers it, "I'd been around him before and he should have known who I was." Not only had she been present in the station when he was being booked; she'd also driven around his neighborhood in a marked car and full uniform. She was afraid he might recognize her. But she didn't realize just how dumb this guy was.

"We met in a motel room that had already been wired for the meeting," McCown says. "About ten officers were waiting for me outside. The gentleman showed up as expected, but he seemed a little leery at first. He questioned me as to whether I was a police officer, and I responded that I was not, so we proceeded to do the deal."

But the dealer's jumpiness continued, increasing Mc-Cown's concerns. Had he recognized her? Was he laying some sort of trap, waiting for her to give herself away?

"This looks like good crack," she said as loudly as she dared. This was the signal to her backup that the dealer had sold her the dope. But had she said it too loud? Something was clearly wrong, because the dealer grew more fidgety than ever. "Yeah, sure," he muttered, his eyes darting around the room as he stowed away his two hundred dollars. "Listen, I gotta go now. Got an appointment on the other side of town."

It turned out she needn't have worried about the dealer recognizing her. He had other things on his mind.

Tests revealed there was hardly any crack in the concoction he sold her. It had been cut with all sorts of weird stuff, but mostly a sugar substitute. It wasn't real cocaine. It wasn't even real sugar. The man had been so embarrassed about the quality of his product and so worried that she would realize how bad it was that he had barely glanced at her.

"I can't believe you did that to me," the dealer blurted when McCown and her colleagues arrested him and confiscated his car—rather, his girlfriend's car.

"I can't believe you didn't know me!" she retorted. "And I can't believe you're selling Equal for $850 an ounce. It's a lot cheaper at the grocery store!"

Hop in Back

54

Officer Lynn Flanders, our Florida friend, had a strange experience with a drunk driver one evening.

"I was pulling over a speeder one night when he put the car in park and jumped into the backseat," she said. "I didn't know if he was going for a weapon or not, so I called for backup.

"In the minute or two that I waited for backup, the couple in the car seemed to be having a fight. They were arguing so loudly I could hear them from my squad car."

When Flanders's backup arrived after a few minutes, she cautiously approached the car she had stopped and peered in the window. A woman sat in the passenger seat with her arms crossed and a furious look on her face.

Flanders asked the woman what she was doing.

"I don't know, Officer," she responded. "Why don't you ask the rocket scientist in the back?"

She gestured toward the disheveled-looking man in the backseat, who looked back with bloodshot eyes.

"Hey, I don't know what's going on," he said with slightly slurred speech and an air of aggrieved innocence. "I've been asleep back here the whole time. Just woke up a minute ago."

"He didn't say that the woman had been driving," Flanders recalls. "If he had, I believe she would have been much harder on him than the courts. So he just went with the ghost-driver theory.

"We ran a check and found out he had several warrants on him. He was arrested for D.U.I."

And poof! Suddenly, he disappeared into the criminal justice system.

Good Thinking

To police officers accustomed to hearing outrageous lies and absurd alibis, a truly honest answer can feel like a breath of fresh air—even if that breath has a distinct smell of alcohol. Captain Don Parker of Pensacola, Florida, received such an answer late one night when he stopped a woman he suspected of driving under the influence.

"By the time I got out of my patrol car," Parker says, "she was already out of her car, staggering back and forth, and obviously very upset with me."

"Why are you stopping me, Officer?" the obviously intoxicated woman drawled before Parker could say a word.

"Well, ma'am, you were weaving all over the road," Parker explained. "And you didn't have your headlights on."

"Oh, I can explain," she replied smartly. "You see, I've been drinking all night, and I'm very drunk."

Parker merely nodded.

"Considering my condition," she finished with unerring and incriminating logic, "I think I'm doing very well."

He had to agree, even as he took her in.

"Oh, I can explain. You see, I've been drinking all night, and I'm very drunk. . . . Considering my condition, I think I'm doing very well."

Read My List

Her second day on the job, a rookie undercover officer in Florida was assigned to purchase some prescription drugs from a known pill dealer. She was given a list of pills to buy and the quantity needed for a good "bust."

"I wasn't familiar with any of them at the time," she remembers. "I had to write down the names of all the drugs and take the list with me."

When the officer arrived at the "Pill Palace" with her shopping list, she began placing her order. "You'd think the dealer might have been a little suspicious since I couldn't tell her what I wanted without consulting my list. I was awful . . . I kept mispronouncing the drugs' names, and she would even correct me."

The suspect sold the officer $250 worth of stolen pills and was arrested moments later.

"I saw her later at the station and heard her asking if anyone had an aspirin. Ironic, isn't it? She had every pill you could imagine, but didn't have an aspirin!"

If You Can't Beat 'Em . . .

Several years ago in Arkansas, a man robbed a pharmacy clerk at knife point. A few days later, the clerk picked the man out of a photo lineup and pressed charges against him. When the case went to trial, however, the man was nowhere to be found. He had fled the state, and officials had no clue where. They knew he came from New York City, but couldn't be sure that was where he had gone, and they didn't know where in New York to look. They really didn't have much hope of catching him.

Then they got the break they needed to find their criminal. Sure enough, the suspect had returned to New York and had applied for a job. Federal authorities were alerted when the man's prints were sent to Washington, D.C., as part of a standard check required for that particular job application. The man was soon arrested, charged, and convicted.

Oh, and he didn't get the job he applied for—that of police officer.

58 Camera Hog

An officer in Indiana told us of a very photogenic crook who insisted on arranging his own close-ups. This criminal specialized in safecracking. He was highly skilled, extremely thorough, and—at the same time—incredibly dumb.

Our safecracking star had targeted a small local business that kept more than seven thousand dollars in cash in a safe. There were no alarms, and the safe was an older model, relatively easy to crack. But when the criminal arrived at "work," he discovered a couple of video surveillance cameras in the building.

That wouldn't do. After all, nobody likes to work with someone watching over his shoulder, right? So our resourceful crook set about making his workplace more comfortable. He found a ladder, climbed up with his screwdriver, and proceeded to take the lens off each camera.

Now, the big problem with most video surveillance is that you really can't get close enough for a really good picture of the criminal's face. The quality is not that good, and the perpetrators are usually too far away for the ceiling-mounted cameras to capture a good image. But our star safecracker took care of that problem for the local police. While he diligently worked with his screwdriver right in front of the camera, he also provided the officers with the best close-up they'd ever seen—right down to the smallest wrinkle and mole. Meanwhile, the camera across the room was providing a full-length view of him working on the first camera.

The video was picture-perfect, and the safecracker was quickly apprehended.

Smile—you're a dumb criminal!

# Another Crime of Passion

It's an age-old story of love, lust, and automobiles—with a new twist brought on by the current Age of Litigation.

A young couple became amorous in a car parked along their town's notorious Lover's Lane. They were in the throes of passion when another car pulled in slowly in front of them. The driver considerately turned off his lights. But then, trying to back up in the dark, the new arrival bumped into the lovers' car.

The couple sued the other motorist's insurance company for child support. The lovers claimed the fender bender outside the car caused another little accident inside the car. The bump from the untimely collision allegedly caused them both to momentarily "lose control"—and the result was an accidental pregnancy.

That's one for the record books—the first and only case (we hope) of a fender bender resulting in a "love child."

Once Bitten, Twice Bitten

Sergeant Doug Baldwin in Pensacola, Florida, was dispatched to assist in a high-speed car chase. He responded immediately and soon was hot on the tail of the speeding vehicle.

Suddenly, the suspect's car veered off to the side of the road. The driver's door sprang open, and the driver bolted from the car. By the time Baldwin could get out of his own car and follow on foot the suspect had disappeared.

A search of the fugitive's car uncovered a quantity of drugs. Now he was wanted for possession, speeding, and resisting arrest. But he was nowhere to be found. An extensive canvass of the area proved fruitless. After hours of searching, the officers were ready to call off the search, but Sergeant Baldwin decided to again check the area.

Looking behind an auto mechanic's shop, Baldwin heard something. It sounded like a man whispering "ouch" and quietly cursing. Officer Baldwin traced the sound to a car up on blocks. He bent down, looked underneath the car, and saw a bare-chested man twitching wildly on the ground.

The officer called to the squirming man, who identified himself as the suspect. "You're under arrest," Baldwin said.

"Okay, but hurry up!" the man pleaded. "You've got to get me away from all these mosquitoes; they're about to bite me to death!"

Sergeant Baldwin dragged the man from under the car and saw that his skin was as bumpy as a rhinoceros's hide from mosquito bites. He handcuffed the suspect and was leading him out of the fenced compound when, from out of nowhere, two security dogs appeared and jumped the bad guy. They bit him several times before Sergeant Baldwin could run them off.

Between the mosquitoes and the dogs, the man had about one hundred bite marks on his body. It was a bad case of "overbite"—and a stellar example of taking a bite out of crime!

All Aboard!

When Nashville police officers Andy Wright and Jeff Cherry observed a possible drug buy in a known high-drug-sales area, they approached the man who had made the buy. But when they began to question him, the criminal struck Officer Cherry in the face and took off running. The chase was on.

For nearly half a mile, the officers pursued the suspect on foot. Then he ran down an embankment and over some railroad tracks into a rail yard, crossing just in front of a long freight train, Cherry said.

Officers Wright and Cherry came to a sudden halt as a train barreled down between the officers and the suspect. Says Cherry, "The train separated us from him, but we knew he couldn't run up the other side because more police were coming from that direction."

The two officers knelt down and watched the unbelievable scene that unfolded.

"Looking under the train, we could see the suspect standing there. We watched him closely because we might lose him if he simply ran next to the train," Cherry said.

Instead, standing perfectly still, this genius reached out and tried to grab the handrail on the train, which was moving at about forty miles per hour. It immediately knocked him to the ground and bounced him about ten feet down the tracks.

"We couldn't believe he did that. It's amazing that his arm wasn't yanked off," Cherry says.

The rocket scientist staggered to his feet and tried to jump on the train again. From a standing start, he just sort of threw his body up against the moving train. It knocked him down once more, only more violently this time. This time he didn't get up. His second attempt to jump the train had left him unconscious.

"We waited another couple of minutes for the train to pass while the suspect just lay there. After the last car went by, we scooped him up and took him to the hospital. They kept him overnight for observation, and he was booked on the following day."

The bad guy now knows the difference between a rail yard and a prison yard. Let's hope he also studies basic physics while he's in the joint.

"We couldn't believe he did that. It's amazing that his arm wasn't yanked off."

Life Is Like a Pair of Brown Shoes

An immigration officer was sick and tired of dealing with illegal aliens who would pretend not to understand any English for several hours and then suddenly speak it fluently. So on this particular evening when the agent stopped a truck filled with thirty illegals, he decided to try something different.

"Do any of you speak English? *¿Habla Inglés?*"

Every head shook no, and every face looked very quizzically at the frustrated officer.

"Okay, well, look, I'm really tired of this. I'm gonna shoot you all, and I'm going to start with the people wearing brown shoes."

As the officer drew his pistol, three men looked down quickly at their feet. They quickly and gladly accepted the role of translator for the group.

The Clothes Make the Man ...Dumb!

63

Dwayne Carver was a maintenance man at the Cedar Wood Apartments in Virginia Beach, Virginia. He had a good job, his own tools, and a blue uniform that read "Cedar Wood" on the back and "Dwayne" on the front.

Now, if you were going to rob a 7-Eleven store, as Dwayne did, you would probably wear a ski mask, as Dwayne did. But you probably wouldn't wear your work uniform . . . yes, as Dwayne did.

When he approached the clerk, his face was completely covered. He even made his voice sound deeper as he ordered, "Give me all the money." The clerk stared at Dwayne and his name tag and handed over several hundred dollars. Dwayne fled to a carefully concealed rental car that he had rented just for the day so that he couldn't be traced.

The police arrived shortly, and the clerk was asked to give a description of the robber. "All I can tell you is that he was wearing a ski mask and a blue maintenance uniform with "Cedar Wood" on the back, and "Dwayne" on the front."

The two officers looked at each other. Surely not . . . no, this was too easy. Maybe the thief stole the uniform or purchased it used at Goodwill. . . .

But it was Dwayne, all right. When the officers appeared at his apartment, he hadn't even changed clothes. The ski mask? It was in his back pocket. The gun? It was in his other back pocket. The money? It was in his front pocket.

You know, this guy's story would have made a great B horror movie back in the fifties. Can't you just picture the title now, slowly dripping down the screen?

Now Showing: The Dwayne with No Brain!

Potted Plants

64

Back in the fifties and the sixties, drugs weren't as prevalent as they are today. And folks in small towns and rural areas were not "hip" to drugs—or so many city dealers and users thought. A dumb criminal with this attitude ran into trouble one day on the main street of a small Indiana town with a not-so-dumb police officer.

Sitting in his squad car just watching traffic on a warm afternoon, Officer Larry Hawkins (not the same Larry Hawkins mentioned earlier in this book) spotted a Ford station wagon with out-of-state license plates—and a rear compartment full of marijuana plants.

"I guess he just figured our little town has a bunch of backward cops who don't know what marijuana looks like," Hawkins said. "Well, I knew what it looked like. I just took off after him, and he didn't run."

The officer pulled the station wagon over and walked

up to the driver's window. "Partner," he said, "I hope for your sake that those plants are plastic."

The man just looked at the officer with a pleasant look on his face and said, "Yeah, they are."

"Well, I'm sure you won't mind if I just kind of check it out."

For a long moment the driver just looked at the woman in the seat next to him. Finally, he shrugged. "Sure."

So the officer went back and opened the tailgate and pulled out seven live marijuana plants—each one in its own pot. They were full-grown plants—the top of each one bent down by the roof of the car. And they were definitely not plastic.

The smart guy was arrested. The sheriff's office used the plants to show schoolchildren what marijuana looks like. And Hawkins had the last laugh on this city slicker.

"They used to make rope out of hemp, which is marijuana," Hawkins says. "This guy had just enough to hang himself."

Once a Soldier . . .

Occasionally, we receive a story here at *America's Dumbest Criminals* headquarters that doesn't involve a dumb criminal, but does involve the police and their ability to defuse potentially volatile situations. There's no criminal in this case, just an unfortunate fellow whose straw, so to speak, didn't go all the way to the bottom of his glass—and an experienced cop who handled a delicate situation with creative efficiency.

"Sometimes an officer has to fly by the seat of his pants," says C. R. Meathrell, chief of the Salem City Police Department in Salem, West Virginia. "And being able to ad lib at the drop of a hat can be a real plus."

Several years ago, when Meathrell was a sergeant working the night shift, he was called to a rest home to take care of a disturbance. An elderly patient had refused to take his medication and had mentally reverted to his days as a private in the army. The old soldier had raised enough pure hell that everyone on his floor was awake.

For well over an hour he had paced the hallway, ranting and raving about the expected German attack. The home had called the police to help them with a transfer to a nearby hospital.

"I had a rookie with me who was still trying to find his way around our little town," Meathrell remembers, "and all the way there he was plotting how we would take this guy. I had to remind him that it was just an old man with a bolt or two loose, not a Charles Manson."

When the officers arrived, staff members were waiting to escort them to the old fellow's room. When the rookie and the uniformed sergeant entered the room, the old man stared at the sergeant's rank stripes and then snapped to attention.

"Sergeant," he blared, "I've been a good soldier. Let me show you my medals." With that, he popped open a cigar box with several figurines in it.

Here's my chance, Meathrell thought.

"Private," he barked, "we are here to get you out of enemy territory. But we must hurry; the enemy isn't far behind."

The elderly "private" snapped to attention again, gathered his duffel bag, and marched out the door.

All the way down the hallway, the sergeant called cadence, and the little group marched out the front door as

The elderly "private" snapped to attention again, gathered his duffel bag, and marched out the door.

if they were going to war. Five or six elderly ladies cheered. One elderly gentleman simply muttered, "Nut."

Things went well until the officers and their charge emerged from the door of the rest home. There the good "private" stopped dead in his tracks. He had spotted the fire department ambulance that stood waiting to transfer him. An attendant opened the side door and offered him a hand, but he wasn't having any part of it.

"It's okay, private," the sergeant assured him. "That's a tank I ordered to get you safely across enemy lines. I'll stay behind and guard our flank."

Like a shot, the good old soldier was up and in the ambulance. Meathrell closed the door and waved good-bye.

As the ambulance drove away, the rookie turned to the sergeant with a slack jaw. "A tank?" he asked in disbelief.

"Don't gripe," the sergeant said. "He's on his way, isn't he?"

A Shining Example

To some people, image is everything. There are those who would not dream of leaving the house (even someone else's house) without making sure their appearance was in order. And different people have different priorities when it comes to appearance. Some people can't relax unless their hair is neatly combed. Others want to be sure their clothes are in style. For Cecil Warren, shiny shoes were everything.

Cecil was well known on the streets of Roanoke, Virginia, as a small-time thief and occasional burglar. He was just as well known for constantly shining his shoes. It wasn't uncommon for him to put on the spit and polish several times a day. In the end, his particular form of vanity proved to be his downfall.

Cecil had decided to burglarize a house, and he had no trouble getting in. He simply climbed up and over the back porch. Unfortunately, this feat also required him to scramble onto the roof. And roof climbing, as one prosecutor later put it, creates "a great probability of shoe damage." Our vain criminal couldn't get on with the job until he made some repairs.

Cecil escaped from the home with some five thousand dollars' worth of jewelry, but he left behind his can of shoe polish and, more importantly, his *monogrammed* shoeshine rag.

"The can of polish and that rag with the initials C. W. on it were as good as a set of fingerprints," one detective noted.

The vain Mr. Warren was found guilty of breaking and entering and grand larceny. He is now cooling his heels—and probably shining his shoes—in jail.

Always Wear Your Seat Belt

Like any safety-conscious motorist, West Texan Dwight Ketchum put on his seat belt before driving off. Nothing wrong with that, except for the fact that the car he was driving away wasn't his. When the police spotted him, Dwight took flight. The police gave chase.

After a few minutes of weaving through traffic at high speeds and still not being able to shake the police, Ketchum decided to bail out from the stolen vehicle. Pulling over, he flung open the car door and attempted to get out and run. But try as he might, he couldn't free himself from the seat belt.

The police were closing in on him fast. Too fast. Our car thief was apprehended while he was still struggling to get out of the stubborn seat belt.

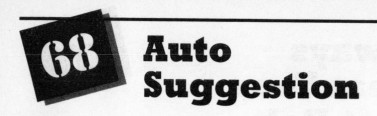

68 Auto Suggestion

When police officers in a Louisiana city arrived at a vehicle accident call involving property damage, the driver was still on the scene, but not exactly "with it."

In a state of heavy inebriation, Montel Stenson told police that he had simply lost control of his European luxury car. During this momentary lapse, it seemed, he had wiped out an entire fence and slammed into a pole.

Officers on the scene were proceeding through their usual drunk-driver routines when Stenson suddenly went berserk. Running back to his automobile, he started it and began ramming one of the squad cars. Backing up and then hurtling forward, he continued to bash the police vehicle. He succeeded in pushing it up against a nearby garage before police were able to extract him.

What was the reason for this bizarre attack? Stenson told police that his European-made automobile had told him to kill the American-made car.

"I was just following orders," was Montel's truly dumb defense.

You've Come a **69** Short Way, Baby

With all the justified focus on violence against women today, inevitably, there had to be a twist, and *America's Dumbest Criminals* found one in Milwaukee. Hardworking thirty-four-year-old Bjorn Svenson had a tough day on the job. His back hurt, his head hurt, and his exhausted legs felt like wet spaghetti. So he expected sympathy when he told his wife that he was just too tired to attend a rally with her later that evening. Being the long-suffering male martyr that he was, he insisted she go on by herself. "Just don't worry about me."

And that's when she hit him.

"She must've hit me twenty times before I finally blacked out," Svenson said later, after regaining consciousness. "I had just finished telling her that I wasn't going and sat down to take my shoes off. That's when she came up behind me, throwing lefts and rights."

He probably wishes that he had gone to the rally with his wife that night. Badly battered Bjorn suffered multiple injuries from the salvo of fists that rained on him during the surprise assault—a broken nose, a fractured skull, a fractured cheekbone, damage to his cornea, and severe cuts and bruises.

The subject of the rally that night was the problem of domestic violence.

DUMB CRIMINAL QUIZ NO. 367

How well do you know the dumb criminal mind?

While robbing a gas station, the attendant asked the robber for a favor, and the robber complied. Did the attendant ask him . . .

(a) to hem his pants?
(b) to let him make one phone call?
(c) to play the guitar accompaniment for "Dueling Banjos"?
(d) not to rob the store?

If you answered (b), then you know the criminal mind. The attendant at the Reno, Nevada, gas station was nothing if not bold. "Remember," he told the man who was holding him up, "every victim is allowed one phone call." The robber agreed, and the attendant called the police. Before you could say "reach out and touch someone," the Reno police were asking that dimwitted robber to do *them* a favor: "Would you put your hands in these cuffs, please?"

Don't Pull That One on Me

Although excuses for speeding are more numerous than pocket protectors at a slide-rule competition, this excuse just didn't add up. When an officer clocked a woman driving in excess of twenty miles per hour over the speed limit, he pulled her over.

He leaned into the driver's side window and observed the female driver of the car clutching painfully at her jaw. She mumbled to the officer. "I'b just cum from da dntest an wud goink homb ta git ma med-cine."

After about ten minutes of painfully slow translation, the officer finally deduced that the woman was speeding because she needed pain medication after a long session with her dentist. For some reason, the officer just wasn't buying her story.

"Maybe I better run a check on your license," the officer said, setting his bait. "I seem to remember a woman with this name who was wanted in an armed robbery."

The woman's eyes grew huge and indignant, and her

mouth flew open. "Why, I have never been so insulted in all my life. How dare you accuse me of being a common—"

Then her hand flew to her mouth as she realized she had spoken very quickly and very articulately . . . and that the officer was not likely to overlook her very rapid emergence from the effects of the Novocain.

She was right.

The officer gave her a "tibket"!

Left Holding the Bag

One balmy Florida evening, Officer Joe Briggs noticed a car weaving down the road. The radio was blaring and the heavy bass vibrated the windows in Joe's cruiser. When the driver of the sound machine crossed the double, solid, yellow center line, Joe had seen enough. He popped on his lights and pulled the vehicle over.

The driver failed every field sobriety test in a laughable manner. He was arrested on a D.U.I. charge. His female passenger, however, was released and free to go. The arresting officer called dispatch to phone a friend of the passenger to come get her. But while he was calling he noticed that she bent down, retrieved a small plastic bag from the hem of her pants, and quickly stuffed it down her blouse.

The officer now needed a female officer to search the suspicious passenger. But while he was making that call, the passenger made a run for it. The officer tackled her before she got too far, clapped her in handcuffs . . . and noticed the several other plastic bags of marijuana that had fallen out of her pocket while she ran.

She was arrested for possession of an illegal substance because she had more than one ounce of marijuana . . . and less than an ounce, apparently, of smarts.

72 The Wrong Guy

A man who had been involved in a hit-and-run . . . ran. He knew he was drunk, and he also knew that getting caught would mean a second conviction of driving under the influence. So he got out of his vehicle, stumbled to the next intersection, and flagged down a car at the stoplight.

"I've been in an 'accidentally,'" he drunkenly explained to the driver. "I need somebody to drive me home."

The driver of the car looked at him thoughtfully. "All right," he finally said. "Get in."

The intoxicated hitchhiker couldn't believe his luck. How often do you find such a willing accomplice on the first try? After just a few fumbles he got the car door open and climbed in beside his Good Samaritan.

But then the drunk man noticed something was wrong. True, his head was spinning. But he could swear that the driver had immediately made a U-turn and headed back in the direction of the accident.

"Hey, man, what are you doing?" he asked weakly.

The undercover cop reached under the seat and pulled out his identification and badge.

"Buddy," he said, "this just isn't your day."

73 **When You Gotta Go**

Captain Pete Bell of the Pensacola (Florida) Police Department was patrolling a nice suburban area when a speeding car ran a stoplight right in front of him. Captain Bell gave chase.

When he had the car pulled over, he approached the driver's side and prepared to write out the ticket. "Sir, I'm going to have to give you a citation for running a red light and speeding."

"Yeah, I know," the man said. "But I've gotta go! I've gotta go!"

Bell was a little taken aback at this guy's apparent lack of concern, even if he was in a hurry to get somewhere.

"Well," Bell said, "you're going to have to wait until I write this ticket."

"I know," the man exclaimed, "but I've gotta go—I've gotta go!"

"Sir, what's your hurry?" the officer questioned.

"Oh, I've gotta go!" came the groaned reply.

"I know you've gotta go—but where?" asked Bell.

"I've *really* gotta go," the man screamed, one arm involuntarily clutching his abdomen. "I have diarrhea. I don't think I can hold it any longer."

Suddenly realizing the situation, Bell quickly tore off the ticket and handed it to the man.

"Here, sir. There's a restroom right across the street at that service station. Have a nice day."

Well, at least now the guy had something to read while he was in the bathroom.

**Go Figure . . .**

An officer in Florida told us about a dumb criminal who showed up too late to be caught in a "sting"—but still managed to work his way into jail:

"The sheriff's department had set up a fake pawnshop that bought stolen goods. We videotaped all our transactions for several months, then shut the whole operation down and arrested thirty or forty people who had sold things to us. That sting attracted national attention, and the press was having a feeding frenzy—almost non-stop coverage—because the audio and video were so good. We recovered everything from sets of silverware to an eighteen-wheeler."

About a week after the pawnshop sting had been closed, sheriff's department personnel went in to unload their equipment and dismantle the operation.

"We arrived in an unmarked cruiser car that, of course, clearly looked like a police car, with antennas and all. We used a huge truck from the jail with the jail's name

Then the bearded man reached into his pocket and pulled out three stolen Social Security checks. "I'll sell these to you for ten cents on the dollar."

printed on the side, two guards, a couple of prison trustees to do the hard labor, and a couple of plainclothes deputies."

They pulled up to the "pawnshop" to find a bearded man sitting on the front steps. He looked at the entourage, recognized one of the undercover agents who had worked the operation, and signaled him to come over.

The agent strolled over to the guy and asked, "What's up?"

"Where've you been?" the bearded man asked.

"We've been around. Why?"

Then the bearded man reached into his pocket and pulled out three stolen Social Security checks. "I'll sell these to you for ten cents on the dollar."

Needless to say, they soon had that man in handcuffs. But as they were putting him in the squad car, the officer couldn't resist asking him a question.

"Didn't you recognize the police units and the security guards and the truck with 'County Jail' on the side?"

"Well, yeah," the dumb criminal answered. "But I just figured you'd stolen the truck and were bringing it down here to sell."

Stop That Thief and Step on It!

A nervous crook sat at an Illinois tavern knocking back beers to "get up his nerve." The beer only managed to shut down his brain while the crook's body went out to rob a nice home. Totally anesthetized, our crook set about breaking into a beautiful ranch house. He tried to pry open a sliding glass door, but he used too much force and broke the glass, cutting himself in the process. The occupant of the house, an older woman who was a very sound sleeper, didn't hear a thing.

Finally, the dumb criminal managed to let himself into the basement. But then he realized he had dropped his flashlight in the yard and couldn't see a thing. Feeling his way around and bumping his shins with almost every step, he managed to find some laundry to tie around his cuts and then to feel his way up the stairs to the first floor.

By now the poor burglar was tired, bleeding, bruised, and still very drunk. He still wanted to rob the house, but first he needed a minute just to lie down and rest. So he felt his way along the walls of the hallway, slowly opened a door, felt his way in at coffee-table height, and finally located an open area where he could lie down. Unfortunately, he got a little too relaxed and soon succumbed to slumber.

At two in the morning the householder woke up and felt a need to visit the bathroom. She swung her legs around to the floor, felt for her slippers, stood up . . . and stepped right on the face of the burglar, who had chosen the floor beside her bed for his nap. He was so far gone that he didn't even stir.

The old saying, "Let sleeping thieves lie," did cross the lady's mind. On second thought, she called the police and had the bumbling intruder arrested anyway.

The Twenty-Eight Daze of February

76

Paul Marguiles, a Nashville police officer, gave *America's Dumbest Criminals* this story about a man with a short-term memory about long months:

On February 25, 1995, Marguiles and his partner stopped a car with a temporary license plate on it in a known drug-traffic area. In Tennessee a temporary tag, as it is known, is made of paper and carries a handwritten expiration date on it. Upon closer examination, they noticed that the tag had been altered from its original expiration date of 2-17-95.

"It did look quite convincing," Marguiles recalls. "The problem was that he had changed the date from 2-17-95 to 2-37-95. It doesn't take a math major to realize that there are only twenty-eight days in February, not thirty-seven."

A search of the vehicle yielded some crack cocaine and a small pipe used to smoke the drug. The car was confiscated, and the driver was arrested for simple possession of a controlled substance, alteration of an auto tag (which is a felony), and driving with a suspended license.

The driver was especially upset when he realized the crack was in the car.

"The car was pretty messy," Marguiles says, "and he apparently didn't realize the stuff was even there."

The only reason he had taken the car out in the first place, he told officers, was that he really needed to buy some drugs.

Name-Brand Robbery

77

A woman who walked into a Mid-Am Bank in Bowling Green, Ohio, and demanded money from the three tellers inside didn't seem like much of a threat at first. She didn't brandish a gun or threaten anyone with violence, according to Bowling Green Police Chief Galen Ash. (There were no customers in the bank, just the tellers and one bank officer.) She was just an average-looking middle-aged woman, with nothing really desperate or criminal about her appearance or demeanor.

But then, suddenly, the stakes went up. The woman repeated her demand for money and brandished a small hand-held device. She claimed it was a radio remote control that at the touch of a button would detonate a car bomb outside, leveling the bank and killing them all. The bank employees glanced nervously at one another. It was not a threat to be taken lightly . . . or so it seemed.

Suddenly, one of the tellers grew surprisingly and defiantly bold. "I'm not giving you anything," she said as she walked out from behind the counter to confront the would-be bank robber. This courageous teller was quickly joined by her two associates, who jumped the woman, wrestled her to the ground, and held her there until the police arrived.

What made the tellers think that the woman wouldn't detonate the bomb?

According to Ash, "I think their first clue was when they saw 'Sears' on the end of the garage door opener."

Gone Fishin'

A retired sheriff from a sleepy little town in East Tennessee told us this story of the famous Greenback Bank. Yes, that is really its name, and the bank was famous for it. It was also famous for the apparent ease by which it could be robbed. The bank had been hit so many times that at one point they had considered installing a revolving door. Several sweet older ladies worked there, and they never put up a fight or made a fuss, so the bank was famous among criminals for being "easy pickings."

But although the Greenback Bank was easy to rob, it was not that easy to get away from. You see, the bank stood on the main road, and that road was the only way in or out of town. Those sweet older ladies would give the robber the money, then just watch which way he or she went. The police would have a roadblock up and the money back in the bank before the frustrated robbers could think of three ways to spend it.

Well, knowing this, a local fishing guide decided he would try a new approach. He would rob the Greenback Bank on foot, and by the time the police arrived he'd be long gone.

So he did. And he was. The fisherman-robber actually got away clean.

Now, knowing the area like he did, he believed that he had found the perfect hiding place for his loot. He stashed the money in the hollow of an old tree that had grown for years by the riverbank.

He decided to wait until spring before retrieving the stolen loot so that no one would suspect when he "came into some cash." Snug in his cabin, he watched the snow and ice come and then melt away, completely unaware that his money was gradually being withdrawn from the "creek bank." All that thawing had caused the river to rise and flood the riverbank. Now the current was gradually washing away all his money.

That spring provided a bonanza for trout fishermen downstream, who were amazed to begin reeling in truly "big ones." The fishing guide's business, on the other hand, quickly slumped. Who needed a guide when everyone in town could tell where to catch twenty, fifty, and hundred-dollar bills?

Before long, the river was filled with would-be trout fishermen who had learned of the unusual way the stream had been stocked. But the authorities eventually found the source of the muddy money and put two and two together. The robber was eventually caught and convicted.

Unlike the money that went downstream, he went up the river.

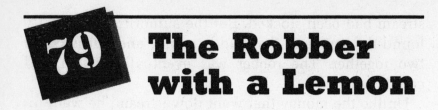

79 The Robber with a Lemon

The Greenback Bank has been robbed many times over its eighty-year history, but the staff will never forget one particular robber. He wasn't particularly bright or very violent, but he did have a remarkable car.

The robber came in with a pistol and demanded money. The tellers smiled pleasantly, complied with the robber's demands, watched which way the robber turned, then called up the road to warn the gas station attendant. The gas station attendant saw the car speed by and called ahead to the police department, who promptly arrested the suspect.

Actually, it might not even have mattered which way this robber turned. Although the crook was surprised at how quickly he was apprehended, no one else was.

As the officer said, "It's not every day you see a 1961 Red Edsel that screams *Arrest me!*"

There were only two cars like it in the entire state.

176

A Con a Sewer

Gary Michaels of Chicago liked the finer things in life: fast cars, fine art, and expensive jewelry—stuff he couldn't begin to afford. But while peering through the window of the jewelry store, he reckoned his luck was about to change. This was the heist that would get him out of the hole.

Simple: Smash the window, grab the jewelry, and run. Quickly, Michaels spotted a street manhole cover. He pried out the one-hundred-pound disk, hauled it to the window, and heaved it through. Michaels grabbed all the rings, watches, and diamonds he could carry, then took off running. Turning the corner, he almost bowled over a couple doing some late-night window shopping. Panicked, he bolted back into the street, heading for an alley, and then disappeared from sight ... down the open manhole.

The Case of the Beer-Box Bandit

Most crooks who set out to rob a convenience store plan on some sort of disguise, such as a ski mask or even a nylon stocking, to hide their faces and avoid being recognized. But one bandit in East Tennessee wore none of the above. He created his disguise right there on the spot.

Retired officer David Hunter of the Knox County Sheriff's Department remarks that this criminal "had a plan, but his plan just wasn't too deep. He had forgotten to bring along a mask." But then he saw it—an empty cardboard beer box!

The robber entered the convenience store with gun in hand and the beer box over his head. He could just barely see out of the corner of it when he turned the empty case at an angle.

After smacking his knee on the door and knocking over several displays, the man finally managed to face the clerk and demand all the money. She put the money in his hand, and he stumbled and crashed his way out the door.

The robber entered the convenience store with gun in hand and the beer box over his head. He could just barely see out of the corner of it when he turned the empty case at an angle.

The man ran out and hurried to his getaway car, driven by his girlfriend. But she, too, seemed to have difficulty thinking clearly under pressure. When the bandit told her to turn right and head out of town, she turned left and was met by about fifteen sheriff's deputies. She almost literally ran into them. Although it was ten o'clock at night, she had neglected to turn on her headlights.

The clueless couple was captured, then released on bail. And about a week later the aspiring criminal hit on another brilliant plan: He would hit the very same market with the same disguise. The police would never expect it and this time, he'd do it right. Then people would remember him—that daring Beer-Box Bandit.

As it happens, the same clerk was working the night the bandit made his second attempt. She recognized him by his box; the door was locked and the sheriff's department was on its way before the bandit could even enter the store.

It's hard to get away with a box on your head . . . and this dumb criminal didn't. His career in crime was over. And yes, we still remember him—that incredible idiot, the Beer-Box Bandit.

Skid Row

When Bob Ferguson, now a retired police officer in Indiana, responded to a burglary call from a gun store, he learned that the thief had stolen thirty rifles, several handguns, and a number of shoulder holsters, then made a clean getaway. There were no witnesses, no surveillance cameras, and virtually no clues. It seemed this case would be chalked up as a loss.

But Ferguson noticed a set of skid marks on the road where someone had obviously peeled out. He followed his instincts and the skid marks. They led him to a corner, where he found another set of skid marks. Farther up the road were another. The marks mysteriously ended in front of an apartment building. Ferguson entered the building, looked around, and headed upstairs.

Outside the door to an upstairs apartment the officer discovered a leather loop that looked exactly like the leather loop on his own shoulder holster. He knocked on the door, and a man in his early twenties answered.

Ferguson poked the leather loop in the suspect's face. "Where did you get this?"

The suspect responded without a blink, "From breaking into the gun store."

Ferguson's quick thinking and the criminal's quick answer led to quick justice—and a whole new meaning to the phrase, "Keep me in the loop."

Back Door Man

Detectives Ted McDonald and Adam Watson of the Brunswick (Georgia) Police Department had taken in a suspect for questioning about a recent homicide. But during the entire interrogation, which lasted several hours, McDonald found himself staring at the suspect's primary identifying feature—his hat.

"I couldn't take my eyes off it," the detective remembers. "It was so big and colorful—I'd never seen anything like it. I kept getting visions of Carmen Miranda in drag. Weird. I guess that hat was his trademark or something.

The detectives felt pretty sure the man with the hat knew more than he was telling, and they suspected he was covering up for some of his buddies. But they didn't really have anything to hold him on, so they finally told him he was free to go. They also told him they were going to talk to his girlfriend to verify his alibi for the night of the murder. He had told them she would support everything he'd said.

"That's cool, man," he said. "You mind takin' me with you when you talk to her?"

Needless to say, the answer was no. The officers wanted to talk to her independently.

"Well, then, can I at least get a ride home?" he asked.

The detectives knew the suspect and his girlfriend both lived in the projects, and he didn't have a car. "Sure," they said, "we'll drop you off at your place, but you can't talk to your girlfriend before we do."

After taking the hat man home, the detectives drove six blocks over and began looking for the girlfriend's apartment.

"It took us a few minutes to find her place," McDonald's partner, Adam Watson, says.

As soon as the detectives knocked, they heard a commotion coming from behind the door—bottles being knocked down, furniture being tripped over, hurried footsteps, and then the slamming of the back door. The man's girlfriend answered the door and gave them permission to enter. But before they began to question her, something in the center of the living room caught their eye.

It was the hat—Carmen Miranda's hat, or, rather, the suspect's hat, left on the table in his haste to beat it out the back door. In the course of five minutes the hat man had run six blocks to his girlfriend's, come in through the back door, told her what to say, and then run out again.

Pretty impressive . . . except for the hat part. Now they knew for sure that he'd been there.

His girlfriend, being smarter than he was, didn't want any part of his lies. She wouldn't corroborate anything he said.

"I think she had just about had it with this joker anyway," McDonald says.

The man was rearrested and, as it turned out, knew more about the homicide than he had let on. The case was later solved.

McDonald sums it up: "He might have had a chance with her if he hadn't left that one-of-a-kind hat sitting on the table. Once we saw that, she couldn't have lied to us if she had wanted to.

"It's funny, though. Every time I see an old Carmen Miranda movie . . . I think of that guy."

Step by Step

If we were stupid enough to risk jail or prison by breaking into a business and stealing something, we'd go for something big, and we'd take every precaution to cover our tracks. But we're not that stupid. That's why we're writing a book and a certain man in Wisconsin is writing his wife.

It had snowed off and on for most of the day. There wasn't a lot of moisture in the air, but there was enough to keep the snow from being blown away by the gusty winter wind.

Toward evening, the police received a call on a 2-11, a burglary. When they arrived at Bernie's Barbershop, they saw that the window had been broken out in the front of the small free-standing building. There really wasn't that much in there to steal. It was a modest two-chair shop.

Bernie the barber was called down to the shop to meet with the officers and take a look at the damage.

"Can you tell us what's missing from your shop, sir?" a young uniformed officer asked the man.

"What's the matter with people today?" the barber mused disgustedly. "I'm a working stiff. What's some jerk doing stealing from a working man?

"Sure, I can tell you what's missing, Officer," Bernie steamed. "My brand new portable color television set that I haven't had long enough to even have to dust yet—that's what's missing! I'd just like to know where the bum that took it is right now!"

It didn't take the officers long to find the answer.

While Bernie talked with the officers, one of the detectives on the scene had discovered something. Footprints. Not the footprints of the officers and Bernie; they were all mixed together in front of the store. No, these footprints led away from the others. Around the corner, past the row of dilapidated houses that lined the block, and down the snowy sidewalk.

Pedestrian traffic had been light that evening, so this particular set of prints was easy to follow. They continued across the street and down the opposite sidewalk. The detective followed them. The uniformed cop followed the detective. Bernie followed the officer.

The prints led to an apartment complex, then to a door, and disappeared behind it. The detective rapped sharply on the door. After a short wait, a nervous woman appeared.

"Yes?" her voice quavered. The detective was looking down. A set of wet footprints still covered the carpet and led right to a large sofa where an even larger man sat watching a hockey game on Bernie's TV.

The reception on Bernie's stolen television was perfect. The only snow was on the man's shoes, the only fuzziness was between his ears. And before the game was over, the larcenous hockey fan was looking at a different station . . . the police station's penalty box.

Dressed for Arrest

Sergeant Larry Bruce told *America's Dumbest Criminals* about a routine warrant he served one morning that took an unexpected twist and became a comedy of errors.

There had been a string of burglaries in the city of Brunswick, Georgia, and Bruce had been put on the case.

"I had a pretty good idea who the person was," Bruce says. "In a town of just seventeen thousand people, if you've been around for a while, you get to know what's going on and who's doing it."

When Bruce had collected all the evidence he needed, a warrant was issued for the suspect's arrest. Sergeant Bruce and another officer set out early on a February morning to serve the warrant. They were hoping to save some effort by catching the suspect while he was still in bed.

"It was exceptionally cold that morning—about twenty-eight degrees," Bruce recalls. "My partner and I walked up the crooked sidewalk to the front door of the man's mother's house. 'This shouldn't be too hard,' I remarked to my partner.

"Well, his mother answers the door and tells us that her son is already up and in the bathroom. So we explained that we needed to talk to him, and would she be kind enough to go and get him for us. Which she did. She returned a moment later with her son right behind her. He wore white jockey shorts, and his face was covered with shaving cream.

"As soon as he saw us he 'booked.' We couldn't believe it at first. The guy runs to the back of the house and out the bathroom window—in his underwear at twenty-eight degrees!"

Still shaking their heads, the officers ran to the squad car to radio for help.

"*In foot pursuit of a black male . . . six-foot-two . . . about one hundred and ninety pounds . . . wearing white Fruit of the Looms and a face full of shaving cream . . . send all available units.*"

The dispatcher was incredulous. "We didn't copy all that. Please repeat."

Bruce repeated the bulletin. Midway through, he realized how it must sound and began to laugh. It took a minute or so to repeat the information. By then both officers were laughing.

"In foot pursuit of a black male . . . six-foot-two . . . about one hundred and ninety pounds . . . wearing white Fruit of the Looms and a face full of shaving cream . . . send all available units."

After a few more minutes, several units had arrived in the neighborhood and an intensive search had begun. As the officers combed the neighborhood, people were coming out for their morning papers.

"Y'all looking for a crazy man runnin' around in his underwear?" one old man asked.

"Yes, we are. Have you seen him?"

"Just turned the corner to the left," he responded with a cackle. "Don't worry 'bout him. He was movin' too fast to freeze!"

The officers turned another corner. A woman in a housecoat stood pointing to a vacant house on a corner lot.

The officers converged on the house, and Bruce knocked. The door swung open. There stood the suspect, still in his undies, and still wearing the shaving cream, which by now had dried out a little. He yawned innocently, stretched, and said, "You looking for someone, Officer?"

"Yes, you!"

The man protested that he had just awakened and was shaving when the officer knocked. The fact that there was no furniture, no running water, no electricity in the house didn't really seem to bother him. Neither did the fact that everybody in town knew the house had been empty for more than a year.

The suspect, now shivering, was escorted to the closest squad car. Bruce and his partner headed around the block to their own unit.

"No, Larry," laughed the other officer as he turned up the collar of his jacket against the cold. "That wasn't hard at all."

Four-Wheel Suspicion

Patrolling a strip of fast-food restaurants in Memphis, two officers spotted a known car thief pulling out from a drive-through window in a car they suspected didn't belong to him. At about the same time, the suspect spotted the patrol unit.

He took off. The cops hit their lights and sirens and started the pursuit.

"We are in pursuit . . . possible stolen vehicle . . . southbound on Washington . . . now heading south onto Adams Street."

"This kid was runnin'," remembers Sergeant Keith Haney of the Memphis Police Department. "We'd dealt with him on numerous occasions in the past, but he was still a minor then, and the courts would let him off easy. He knew this, so whenever he'd steal a car, he would always go for broke when he was being chased by the police. He was a real cocky kid, too. But this was the first time we'd ever been after him since he turned eighteen. Now he was an adult—and could be tried as one."

"Suspect just took out part of a fence at Garden and Greenlawn and is now going the wrong way on Lincoln Avenue."

This was one car thief who was determined not to be caught. For a good twenty minutes he sped through stop signs and red lights, down side streets and back alleys. Finally, surrounded by police units, he abandoned the car and attempted to flee on foot. The officers caught him before he had run twenty yards.

The next day, the new adult was taken to Haney's office for questioning.

"You've got the wrong man," the kid stated boldly. Apparently, he had spent the long night in jail strategizing about how he was going to get out of this one.

"Really?" the sergeant responded. He glanced down at the arrest record. "They identified you in a car that didn't belong to you, chased you for seven miles, then arrested you right after you exited the vehicle. Of course it was you."

The thief shook his head back and forth. "There's no way they could have identified me," he said cockily.

"And why is that?" Haney asked.

"I was wearing a baseball cap," he sneered. "And the windows of the car were tinted."

Quick Comeback

Officer Dan Leger, a southern undercover narcotics officer, was always quick with an ad lib. One story Leger told us really showed the importance of the quick comeback in police work. A creative impromptu answer can be an officer's best tool for handling the situation by controlling the conversation.

"I was working undercover, and I was making a buy. You've got to record everything you can for evidence when the buy goes down, and this means you almost always have to be wearing some sort of 'wire' for recording your conversations. Unfortunately, every dealer knows that, too. Hollywood has always shown the undercover cop putting a wire right on the chest area, so for starters you want to be creative in where you put the wire. But you've also got to be prepared to talk your way out if the bad guys happen to find it. You'd be surprised at what they'll believe."

One criminal, for instance, went straight to Leger's wire and confronted him, blowing the officer's cover sky high. In less than a minute, however, Leger had managed to convince the criminal not only that he wasn't a cop, but also that he was one of the baddest and smartest criminals that particular dumb criminal had ever run into.

When the criminal shouted, "This is a wire! You're a cop!" Leger looked at him like he didn't have a lick of sense and then explained the facts of life.

"Of course it's a wire," he said patiently. "My lawyer told me to wear this so I'd have evidence to prove entrapment if I ever made a buy from an undercover officer. You ought to be wearing one, man. If a cop busts us and we go to court, it's our word against the cop's . . . and who do you think a judge is going to believe? But if you've got them on tape you can blow their case right out of the water."

The dumb criminal was stunned by the logic.

"Wow, that's really true, man. Great idea! Where did you get yours?"

"I told him where he could get a wire, and I also gave him some tips on how to wear it. He thanked me warmly for the information, then he went ahead and sold me the dope. I eventually proved my point in court."

The judge and jury did take Leger's word over the dumb criminal's because Leger had the recording from his wire and that was the evidence that convicted him.

As the Crow Pries

A burglar alarm went off at the station, and Lieutenant Dewey Betts of the Memphis Police Department quickly rolled out. The alarm was from a drug rehabilitation center Dewey was familiar with. When he arrived on the scene, it was obvious that the burglar had broken in through a second-floor window. What was not obvious was why the burglar chose the center. It's not exactly the logical place for a dumb criminal to look for drugs or money.

Betts called for backup and waited for the arrival of the second unit. Meanwhile, he stood with his back against the wall, hidden, in case the crook looked out and saw him standing there.

There was a creaking noise and the lieutenant looked to the side. The crook was trying to make his escape headfirst through the first-floor window. Not wanting the suspect to get away, the officer grabbed the crook by the collar and started to pull him through the window to the ground where he could cuff him. But when Betts pulled, the burglar screamed uncontrollably.

Betts was stunned at the man's reaction. He thought then that he might have an out-of-control drug addict on his hands. He couldn't let the man go because the suspect was in the kitchen and there were too many possible weapons lying around. So he kept pulling. Every time Betts pulled, the burglar screamed louder and louder.

When Betts's backup arrived, they tried to pull the man through the window . . . with the same results. With every tug, the man screamed at the top of his lungs.

Finally, two of the officers went inside the center, got behind the man, and pushed him out of the window into Betts's arms. That's when the lieutenant noticed a shiny object tucked into the burglar's pants. It turned out to be a chrome-plated crowbar that the crook had used to break into the center.

Now everything became perfectly clear. When the crook was leaning out the window with the crowbar wedged down the front of his pants, he had created a painful leverage on his privates. Every time someone pulled on him, the crowbar would act like a small, effective lever and apply enormous pressure on the suspect's groin area. Since the source of his agony was also important evidence in his crime, he didn't really want to tell the officers, "Guys, there's a crowbar in my pants. Could you stop pulling on me, please?"

Needless to say, the lieutenant didn't need to pry a confession out of this particular dumb criminal.

Stealing Home!

It was the early 1990s and baseball would never again be played in the old Comiskey Park in Chicago. Cheering crowds believed they had seen the last play at the historic stadium. Not long afterward, however, two dumb but nostalgic baseball fans decided to try one last half-inning on their own.

The two men climbed onto the field at night with the intention of stealing the old home plate for a souvenir. Silently, they crept over the field with their shovels, peering nervously over their shoulders, jumping at the slightest sound, but determined to obtain their prize. What a collectible!

But surely they paused for just a moment to contemplate, to look up at the silent, shadowy stands and hear the cheers once more. They must have gazed down at that old plate, envisioning all the runs that had been scored from that spot, all the great batters who had stood there, all the great pitchers who had hurled the ball toward home.

They paused for just a moment to wonder how they were going to get away with their crime now that two security guards were running toward them on the field.

There was a frantic rundown play between third and home before the two thieves were captured for the unofficial final out at the old Comiskey Park.

The Fall Guy

We've all heard of people who have been in accidents that could have or should have killed them but were so drunk they weren't even injured. Detective Adam Watson of Brunswick, Georgia, tells about one of those people whose amazing good luck managed to outstrip his sheer dumbness.

Watson was dispatched to an exclusive resort estate late one Saturday night to check on what was supposed to be a break-in with the suspect still on the premises. The terrified occupants of the house, an older couple by the name of Thompson, had whispered the story over the phone when they called police.

Around midnight, the Thompsons said, a man had appeared at the front door of their residence and begun pounding crazily, determined to gain entrance. Not surprisingly, they had refused to let him in. After several unsuccessful minutes the man had moved to the back door and continued his pounding. Then, as the Thompsons were phoning the police, they heard the sound of shattering glass and a loud thud that told them their intruder had somehow gained admittance. They didn't try to find out how. They just locked themselves in their bedroom and waited for the police.

"When we arrived," Watson says, "we began an immediate search of the home with weapons drawn. We came around the corner and entered a hallway on the first floor. And there in a crumpled heap lay the intruder— out cold. But it wasn't until much later, when we got him to the hospital and he woke up, that we were able to piece together what really happened."

The burglar, it turned out, wasn't really a burglar. He was a high-powered executive who had been visiting friends at the resort. That night, he had gotten totally wasted in a local bar and then gotten lost. Drunk and unfamiliar with the area, he arrived at the Thompsons' and assumed their home was the condo where his friends were staying. He had beaten frantically on all the doors, seeking admission.

Getting nowhere, he had next decided to scale the side of the house and climb in through a second-story window. First he tried to open it, then finally he smashed it and fell through.

Unfortunately for him, the window he chose was in a room with a cathedral ceiling. There was no second floor to land on. He fell twenty feet and landed in the first-floor hallway.

When the intruder was finally able to talk to police the next day, he told them that all he remembered was knocking on the door. He had no recollection of climbing up the house or falling twenty feet or being arrested—he was just too drunk to remember anything at all.

"We ended up charging the guy with criminal trespassing," the officer states. "There was nothing else we could charge him with. He really wasn't breaking in, and there was no criminal intent."

And amazingly, the only ill effects he seemed to suffer from his twenty-foot fall were a few bruises.

DUMB CRIMINAL QUIZ NO. 457.2

How well do you know the dumb criminal mind?

A dumb crook tried to rob a gas station, but the attendants didn't cooperate. When neither attendant would hand over the money, did the criminal . . .

(a) **start crying and run away?**
(b) **challenge the attendants to an arm-wrestling contest for the money?**
(c) **threaten to call the police?**
(d) **hold his breath until he passed out?**

If your answer was (c), then you're getting the idea. A would-be bandit in Oklahoma grew so upset that the gas station attendants refused to give him the money that he threatened to call the police. When the attendants still refused, the man made good on his threat. Needless to say, he was half-gassed himself at the time.

Wrong Side of the Tracks

No officer likes to get a call involving a train accident. They are usually the bloodiest and most disgusting scenes imaginable.

One evening Marshal Larry Hawkins of Little Rock got a call that a pedestrian had been hit by a train. Expecting the worst, Hawkins reported to the scene. He arrived to find a crowd of spectators craning their necks to get a better look. The marshal elbowed his way through the crowd and saw the victim—standing up talking to someone and brushing off the dirt on his pants.

Here's the story Hawkins unraveled: The man and his wife were at Johnson's Tavern, which is right next to the railroad tracks. They both got drunk, and then they got into an argument. He said to her, "The hell with you, I'm walking home." The railroad track went right past his house, so he decided he was going to walk the tracks home.

Meanwhile, a southbound train was on its way. And

But the important thing is that he was lying between the two rails when the train went over him.

somewhere between the tavern and home, the train and the drunk man managed to meet.

The conductors and the engineers all saw a man go down, and they were sure the train went over him. They assumed he had been killed. But somehow after the train had managed to stop, the dumb, drunk, and incredibly lucky criminal was still alive.

To this day, no one is sure exactly how it happened. The train might have knocked the man down, or he might have passed out on the tracks. But the important thing is that he was lying *between* the two rails when the train went over him.

Said Hawkins, "Now, there's always stuff hanging down under a train, like air hoses and stuff, and those things did clip him and roll him around. He was bruised, scratched, and cut, and his clothes were torn. But he was all right. He was up and walking around—still drunk and scared out of his mind. I took him in for his own protection and arrested him for public intoxication."

My Name's Steve, and I'll Be Your Dealer Today

Giving one more glance around the crowded bar, Agent Johnson (who's still working undercover in the South somewhere and shall therefore remain otherwise nameless) yawned and sighed. He was working undercover narcotics and had wanted to bust a certain known dealer that night. But the dealer had never appeared. Whatever the reason, the whole evening had been a colossal waste of time.

The agent was about to pay his tab and go home when a man slid onto a stool next to him and struck up a conversation. Johnson began to suspect that this man might also have connections to the drug culture.

"Hey, man," he asked his new acquaintance, "you know where I can buy some reefer?"

The man said evenly, "As a matter of fact, I do." After a few more minutes' conversation, Agent Johnson understood that the man was referring to himself.

By now Johnson was wondering, *How am I going to find out who this guy is?* He had to have a name in order to serve a warrant. And he had to serve a warrant, because to arrest the man on the spot would jeopardize the entire operation and blow his cover as well.

The new suspect didn't feel comfortable selling drugs in the bar, so they strolled outside into the parking lot. The man led Johnson to his car. The agent was still racking his brain, trying to think of a way to learn the dealer's name.

Then the dealer himself solved the problem.

"Listen, man, it's nothing personal," he said. "But I don't know who you are. I mean, you could be a cop for all I know. So can I see your driver's license?"

With a rush of relief, the agent pulled out a phony driver's license that he used for undercover work. And then he said, "Hey, I don't know who you are either. Can I see *your* driver's license?"

"Sure," the dealer replied.

The agent looked at his license, memorized the information, and made the buy. About a week later, the dealer was treated with a personalized warrant for his arrest signed by his new friend, Johnson.

Hooked on Crime

In a Florida town, the first policewoman on the local force was sent undercover to crack down on the prostitution problem. Her particular targets were the "johns," or clients, who are considered as much a part of the problem as the prostitutes themselves. (After all, it's just as illegal to buy it as it is to sell it.)

The police officer was dressed to look like a "working girl," wired for sound, and sent out to walk the streets. It wasn't long before a well-dressed man picked her up.

"Are you a cop?" the man asked her.

"Do I look like a cop?" she responded.

"Well, no, you look too nice to be a cop."

So the conversation continued, and the man eventually told the undercover officer what he had in mind. But that wasn't enough to arrest him for solicitation, however. He also had to offer to pay her.

"What's in it for me?" the officer asked.

"Well, normally," the man said, "I don't pay more than fifty dollars. But as good as you look, I'd pay you a hundred bucks."

The officer leaned down and spoke into her hidden microphone, "Fellows, did you hear that? I knew I could make a whole lot more money doing something besides being a cop."

The man was flabbergasted. "You are a cop!" he yelled.

The female officer looked at him smugly. "Yes, I am."

"Hell!" the man exclaimed. "If you'd have told me you're a cop, I would've offered you two hundred bucks. I've never screwed a cop before."

"You've been screwed by one now," the officer remarked. "You're under arrest."

94 A Red-Hot Robbery

In St. Louis, Missouri, two men entered a convenience store with the intention of robbing it. They made their intention known to the clerk—but they had no weapons. The clerk told them that if they didn't leave the store he would call the police.

Frightened that their robbery wasn't working out like the ones on television, the two crooks made a run for it. But one of the robber wannabes decided he was going to steal *something*—so he grabbed a hot dog off the rotisserie and quickly shoved the whole thing in his mouth.

A few steps outside the convenience store, the hot-dog thief collapsed—he was choking on the frankfurter. Faced with this beautiful case of poetic justice—it takes a weenie to stop a weenie—the other man did the only honorable thing a dumb criminal can do. He ran like hell, leaving his partner gasping in the parking lot.

He grabbed a hot dog off the rotisserie and quickly shoved the whole thing in his mouth.

The Five-Year Cab Ride

Late one evening, in a small town in Illinois, a taxi was called to a local bar to pick up a man who had imbibed a bit too heavily. The gentleman in question staggered out to the cab, gave his home address, and slouched back into the seat as the taxi pulled away from the curb.

When they arrived at the guy's house, the drunk told the cab driver that he didn't have any money on him, but that he had some in the house. "I'll just run in and be right back out with the money, okay?"

That was fine by the cabby; it happened all the time. But not quite this way.

The man got out of the cab, staggered into his house, and reappeared a few moments later.

"I couldn't find any money," he slurred, "but I found my gun, so you're going to have to give me all *your* money."

Believe it or not, this guy actually robbed the cab driver at gunpoint, took the money, and then lurched back into his house, leaving the cabby still parked outside.

You don't have to be psychic to see where this is going. The stunned and shaken cab driver backed his vehicle up about a block, called his dispatcher, and told them he had just been robbed at gunpoint, and then described exactly where the armed robber was at the very moment.

When the police arrived on the scene, the cabby repeated his story to them. Then he watched as the police approached the house, weapons drawn.

Pete Peterson was an officer on the force at the time. He remembers that the front door was wide open when the officers approached.

"Only the storm door was shut," Pete recalls, "and it wasn't locked."

The officers looked in through the storm door to the lighted living room. There on the coffee table was the .38-caliber handgun. And there on the sofa, passed out cold, was the robber.

The drunk was sentenced to five years in prison for armed robbery. He might as well have told the cabby, "Take me straight to jail."

 # Winner Loses

Winning the lottery is every gambler's dream. So when Donna Lee Sobb hit the California state lottery for one hundred dollars she was thrilled. Not only did she need the money, but her winning ticket also qualified her for the big two-million-dollar jackpot.

Things were looking up for Donna, it seemed. She smiled as she looked at her picture in the local newspaper. She was getting some attention, and people on the street occasionally recognized her. Unfortunately for Sobb, so did the people on the beat—the police beat, that is. A local cop read her story, saw her picture, and recognized her as the woman wanted by authorities on an eight-month-old shoplifting warrant.

Now Sobb *really* needed that hundred dollars she had just won. She ended up applying it toward her bail.

The Civic-Minded Cocaine Cooker

It was October 1993 in a Georgia town when Tyrell Church was in the kitchen cooking up his specialty . . . cocaine. He had been doing that for a good thirty years, but he had never seen any that cooked up like this batch. Something was wrong.

"I had never seen powder cocaine that turned red when you cooked it up," Church explained. So, being concerned for his own welfare as well as that of the public at large, Tyrell Church did what any fool would do. He took the suspicious concoction to the Georgia Bureau of Investigation crime lab for analysis.

The lab ran four separate tests. The substance proved to be cocaine after all. And Church was promptly arrested and charged with possession of the same. He opted to serve as his own lawyer in what to him seemed a ridiculous trial.

"Had I known I was going to be arrested," he argued, "I wouldn't have taken it over to the lab."

So why did Church take his cocaine to the lab?

"If kids get hold of something like this," he said, "it might hurt them or poison them. I took it over there to have it tested to see if it had been cut or mixed with any dangerous substances."

The civic-minded cooker went on to say that if something had been wrong with the cocaine, he could have warned the public.

Church insisted that he had often had his cocaine tested in New York, where he once lived.

"What's the sense in having a crime lab," he asked, bewildered, "if a person can't take anything over there?"

He also requested that the substance be retested, a request which the judge denied.

"I'm not a habitual user," the cooker complained in his final statement. "I use cocaine for my arthritis. It's a waste of the taxpayers' time for this kind of case to come to court. The grand jury shouldn't have even bothered."

"I do not think a violation of the cocaine law is a waste of time," the district attorney countered.

The jury couldn't have agreed more. It took just seven minutes for them to return a guilty verdict.

Cold Cash

In Decatur, Illinois, a house had been burglarized by someone familiar with the family—and familiar with where they kept their money. The cash was all in change—rolls of quarters, dimes, and nickels. And kept in the freezer.

During the investigation, one of the detectives was doing the necessary legwork of asking people in the neighborhood if they had seen or heard anything unusual or suspicious the night of the burglary. One person had noticed a car that was parked in the rear of the residence that evening and was able to provide a rather vague description of the vehicle.

Following up on that sparse lead, the investigator stopped by a neighborhood gas station and asked the attendant on duty if he'd seen a car that fit the vague description or seen anyone that might have looked suspicious to him that night.

"Well," the clerk mused, "there was one fella who came in the station that night and paid for his gas in rolled change. I remember because the money was cold, real cold, like it had been in the freezer or something."

Bingo! The detective asked the attendant if he could identify the man if he saw him again.

"Sure, I could," the man stated. "He comes in here about every day or so and buys gas."

The detective handed the clerk his card.

"If that guy comes in here again, I'd like you to get his license plate number."

The very next day the clerk called with the tag number of the vehicle, and the suspect was quickly apprehended."

"Can you believe it?" the detective asks. "I mean, the guy didn't even wait until the money had warmed up before he started spending it—and he only went one block away."

Bloodhound
Blues

During the two years that Dan Leger worked under-cover down South as a narcotics officer, he had more than his share of dumb criminal encounters. And he was constantly amazed at the "cop folklore" circulated among criminals—the widespread misinformation about the law and police procedure. He tells this story about his all-time favorite dope:

"I was working undercover narcotics, deep cover. I looked like the nastiest of the nasties. I infiltrated the in-dependent bikers and tapped into some large distribu-tion systems. Over the course of a few months I made several buys from a fairly large supplier. We got to be pretty good acquaintances."

One night Leger and the dealer were sitting around talking, and the dealer got going on the subject of how undercover cops work. Leger could hardly keep a straight face as he listened to the man's ignorance.

"I can always spot a cop," he bragged, "the way their eyes move around a room and the questions they ask."

Then he went on to relate an old hippie myth that originated in Berkeley or someplace similar. The gist of it was that years ago a city council somewhere decreed that undercover officers had to identify themselves as police officers if they were asked a direct question three times.

"Sort of defeats the purpose of going undercover, you know?" Leger laughs. "Now, if that were the law everywhere, you wouldn't have any undercover officers, because they would all be dead now. But this guy has heard this story, and he lets me in on the secret: 'This is the trick the cops don't want you to know. If you ask an undercover cop three times if they're a cop and they don't tell you, then it's entrapment, and the case gets thrown out.'

"It's really hard to look impressed when inside you're laughing your ass off, but I nod my head like I'm committing his every word to memory.

"Then he did it. He really pissed me off. He said, 'I can smell a cop a mile away.' I was sitting about two feet away from him at the time."

Leger had to bite his tongue to keep from saying something right then, but he knew he'd have the last laugh in the near future. And sure enough, about three weeks later he took that dealer down with a rock-solid case.

"I relished the moment," Leger remembers. "I whipped out my badge and got right up in his face and said, 'Guess what? I'm the Man, and you are under arrest.' His face got as pale as a cadaver, and then I just couldn't resist rubbing it in.

"I was an inch from his nose.

"How do I smell from here?"

100 All's Well That Ends

One rainy night at the state penitentiary in Michigan City, Indiana, three hardened convicts escaped through a dark, muddy field. They had been convicted of everything from armed robbery to murder. Now they were armed and dangerous and had nothing to lose.

They crept up on a dark, still house. The garage door was unlocked, and they walked right into the kitchen. Creeping from bedroom to bedroom, they bound and gagged all four members of the family. One of the criminals rifled through all the jewelry boxes while another found the car keys. The third got the man's wallet for the credit cards. Then they were off.

Back at the prison, a random bed check revealed the convicts' escape. Soon, helicopters, dogs, and numerous state, county, and city units began combing the area. Once the family managed to free themselves and call the authorities, the police had a car description and a tag number.

Within moments a state trooper spotted the stolen family station wagon moving at a high rate of speed on the interstate. He gave chase, and the escapees made a run for it, veering across the grassy median in an attempt to lose the trooper.

As the fleeing car bounced up onto the other side of the highway, the driver lost control. The car rolled three times, and the convict in the backseat was thrown clear into the high grass. Unharmed, he lost no time disappearing into a nearby cornfield.

Two miles away at Ollie Hardison's farm, the silent dawn was shattered by the thundering wash of police choppers overhead and the baying of bloodhounds closing in on a scent. Ollie had several hog sheds out behind his barn that were pretty well rusted out and falling down. He thought he had heard something out there just a moment before, but now he couldn't hear anything for all the commotion.

One of the arresting officers, Larry Hawkins (the one from Indiana mentioned earlier, that is), will never forget the scene that followed.

The fleeing convict had cut through the fields off the interstate, running at top speed through corn nine feet high. When he came upon the dilapidated hog sheds, he tried to get into one. It was too small. But when he heard the choppers and dogs, the desperate man dropped to all fours and backed into the stinking hog shed.

Unfortunately for him, as he backed in, he also backed out. It seems the back of the shed was rusted out to form a perfect picture frame for the convict's posterior, which was totally exposed. As the police encircled the shed, the convict's rear was positioned in a most peculiar way for arrest.

"He really thought he was totally hidden. He looked like an ostrich with his head in the sand. He held perfectly still and we just sort of stared at this big rear end sticking out of that shed. We just had to laugh. We didn't know whether to turn the dogs loose on him, read him his rights, or just give him a good swift kick."

Good sense and professionalism prevailed. The officers and Ollie Hardison were the only ones to get a kick out of the situation. And they did—no ifs, ands, or butts.

"We didn't know whether to turn the dogs loose on him, read him his rights, or just give him a good swift kick."

229

Wanted!
DUMB or ALIVE

WARNING:
THE CRIMES YOU ARE ABOUT TO READ ARE TRUE.
THE NAMES HAVE BEEN CHANGED ...
TO PROTECT THE IGNORANT.

To God, our loving families, and
our friends—in that order

Introduction

Hello. I'm Alan Ray, and he's Daniel Butler. One day we got this crazy idea to write a book about true stories of dumb criminals. Not in our wildest collective dreams did we envision the amount of time, money, laughter, sacrifice, and hard work it would take to bring this quest to fruition.

We were prepared to accept the fact there might not be that many stories out there. What we weren't prepared for was the salvo of funny, absurd, and oftentimes unbelievable stories we would ultimately uncover and put into our first book, which we titled *America's Dumbest Criminals*. We were in awe, and we are still. That book went on to be a surprise bestseller. And it brought to us even more amazing true stories from policemen and policewomen all over the country—one hundred of which appear in the pages of this second book.

The last year has been an incredible time for us. The months and months on the road, the thousands of miles we traveled, our patient families at home, and the hundreds of good people we've been blessed to have met all serve to remind us that the truest reward isn't found in the destination, but in the journey. This journey has given back more in experience, memories, and stories we could tell than it ever took out in the many lean days and sleepless nights we spent trying to make it happen.

Like interviewing seventy-five-year-old retired cop Hi Powell, who once smacked Bugsy Siegel upside the head when Bugsy offered him a bribe. Once, when we were on the road doing a book signing in conjunction with a phone-in radio interview in Birmingham, Alabama, we got a call from a guy in prison listening to the show. He was doing fifteen years for something. He told us a couple of stories, we told him a few, and we all laughed together. Before he hung up, he requested an autographed copy of the book. We figured he probably wouldn't make the book signing the next night (at least, we hoped he wouldn't), so we sent him a signed copy. We were very happy that he had called in because it told us that he understood the humor of it all.

We certainly learned a lot about *dumb criminals*. For one thing, it's a club anyone can join. In fact, if memory serves, one time we were on our way to Pensacola, Florida, to do some interviews. It was probably four in the morning, and we were absolutely fried. We were on a two-lane highway, running sixty miles per hour in heavy fog, when suddenly—I guess we'd reached some little town—the road forked sharply. You could go right, or you could go left. I went straight. I mashed on the brake pedal while giving the seat a hickey at the same time. Daniel awoke from his coma long enough to mutter a catatonic "uh-oh" as we skidded fifty feet to a sideways stop in a parking lot. We were sitting in the parking lot of the Alabama state police headquarters!

Our heads slowly turned toward each other at the same time, like a ventriloquist and his dummy. "Wanna get some stories while we're here?" we asked in unison. We were awake after that and we laughed all the way to Florida. Live and learn.

We've spoken with so many wonderful people we could write a book on just the insightful thoughts and philosophies that policemen and policewomen around the country have shared with us. (Let me make a note of that.) We hope that this second collection of stories about America's dumbest criminals will give you just a taste of what we've experienced.

As in the first book, none of the dumb crimes depicted is still under adjudication. None of the criminals is identified by his or her real name, and some details have been changed to protect the privacy of the people involved. But all the stories are real and so are the cops who appear in this book. We use their real names with their permission. We are especially grateful to Don Parker and Mac Bennett for going above and beyond the call of duty in providing us with so many great stories. Thanks, guys!

It really has been a wild ride—and as far as we can see, it's not over yet. So to God, our families, our friends, the police, our publisher, and to you, we say: Thanks for the journey. We'll see you along the way.

The Bagman Cometh

Disguises often cause dumb criminals a lot of problems. Such was the case with the would-be robber who, according to Lt. John Hutchinson of Little Rock, Arkansas, was captured on surveillance camera video.

It seems our burglar had a carefully thought-out plan to rob an electronics store, but he forgot about his all-important disguise. So just before he entered the store, he grabbed a plastic bag and yanked it down over his head. Mind you, this was not a clear plastic bag, but the opaque garbage variety, and our suspect didn't take the time to cut out eyeholes.

Roll tape, and we see our antihero on surveillance video stumbling through the electronics store, falling over television sets and even tripping an alarm system on display. Finally, he falls to the floor, nearly suffocating on his plastic bag, and crawls to an exit.

But he's back minutes later, this time with two eyeholes cut out. This time he succeeds in grabbing more than sixteen hundred dollars' worth of electronic gear and getting away with all of it, scot-free.

Or so it seems.

After the police stopped laughing at the surveillance footage, they noticed that below the Bagman's clever disguise was a security guard's uniform complete with nametag. He was, they cleverly deduced, the mall security guard who was on duty at the time.

Sure enough, the security guard was setting up his new entertainment center at his apartment when the police arrived. Judging from this brilliant man's past history, we would not be surprised if he came back to rob the store again with a full-length, clear-plastic dry-cleaning bag to cover his uniform.

They're Gonna Get Ya

Detective Jerry Wiley of Birmingham, Alabama, has been involved in a lot of sting operations in his time, but none as outrageously successful as this one. It came about because his department was holding almost three thousand outstanding warrants for crimes ranging from parking violations to assault. Sending out warrant officers to track down each offender and serve each warrant would have taken thousands of man-hours and probably years. So the department decided that instead of going to the criminals, they would get the criminals to come to them.

Here's the sting setup: The police department put together a sports channel for the local cable system—on paper only. The letterhead and promotional brochure bore the phony sports channel's logo, WGGY, which, by the way, stood for "We're Gonna Get Ya." The president of WGGY was "J. L. Byrd," who sent out a letter to each offender explaining that he or she was "already a winner!" All the "winners" had to do was show up at a selected site at a certain time on the day of the drawing for an all-expenses-paid vacation to New Orleans.

The cops had no idea how many people would respond. Commercial direct-mail marketers consider a 10 percent response a huge success for promotions of this type. But on the day of the drawing, the police were stunned to see more than four hundred people already lined up waiting to claim their tickets and win the trip to New Orleans.

All the "winners" were asked to present a photo I.D. and informed that family members could not accompany them into the room where the drawing would be held. They would be processed in groups of twenty-five at a time. (The small groups were necessary to keep the crowd manageable and insure that no one would be injured.)

To keep the crowd entertained and involved as people were slowly being processed, Wiley took a video camera down the waiting line and interviewed the lucky "winners." He even asked some of them to do promos for the new sports channel. Looking right into the camera, dumb criminal after dumb criminal said, "WGGY got me. Did they get you yet?" Meanwhile, the people ahead of them were inside getting the surprise of their lives.

As each group sat down in the winners' room with

Looking right into the camera, dumb criminal after dumb criminal said, "WGGY got me. Did they get you yet?"

their fingers crossed and their hopes high, President J. L. Byrd (actually, a detective from vice) stood behind the podium and explained the drawing. "We're about to give you your tickets and have the drawing for the trip to New Orleans. But first, we have one more surprise for you."

At that instant, the doors burst open with armed S.W.A.T. team officers surrounding the "winners," who immediately put up their hands in utter shock and disbelief. Since it was impossible to pat down the offenders for weapons, the appearance of the S.W.A.T. officers was so sudden that nobody even thought of responding.

The sting succeeded in taking more than four hundred criminals off the streets, collecting more than ten thousand dollars in fines, and saving the city thousands of dollars in door-to-door searches and warrant serving. Not a bad day's work.

Photo Finish

Officer Aaron Graham of Louisville, Kentucky, likes to tell this story of a crime with a photo finish. It began with a woman strolling through a park en route to a company picnic. Swinging from her shoulder was her trusty Polaroid camera, all loaded and ready to catch some candid shots of this wacky annual summer get-together. The sun was setting, and the sky was ablaze with color as a breeze cooled the evening air. It was one of those relaxing evenings when you can't help but let your guard down just a little.

Suddenly, she heard running footsteps. Someone jerked the woman's arm and grabbed the camera. A patrol officer responded to the woman's screams and set out on foot in pursuit of the young thieves. While he ran, he radioed in a physical description of the perpetrators and their general direction of flight.

Meanwhile, in a small wooded grove not a quarter of a mile away, the thieves were checking out the camera. But something was wrong. They took each other's pictures easily enough, but the film that emerged from the camera was black. Disgusted, they tossed the photos and headed for the pawnshop to see what they could get for the malfunctioning camera.

Several police units and several bicycle and horse-mounted officers were close behind, forming a perimeter as our foot patrol officer stumbled into the grove of trees. There, lying at his feet, were the quickly developing Polaroid photos of the culprits. The officer knew he must be less than a minute behind them because the developing process was just finishing.

The two boys were nabbed about a half-mile away as they photographed squirrels. But they were still having problems. They would shoot a photo, look at it, and toss it down, grumbling, "Darn camera doesn't work!"

The trail of photos they left behind worked better than a trail of bread crumbs.

The Name Game

Officer Ed Leach of Birmingham, Alabama, likes to tell the tale of two brothers, Jack and Joe, who greatly resembled each other in both physical appearance and their less-than-brilliant behavior.

Jack and Joe were often getting into trouble of one sort or another, only to weasel their way out of sticky situations by switching identities. If one got nabbed for doing something wrong, the innocent one would use the other's name to get out of trouble. The ploy usually worked, until Officer Leach decided to turn the tables while trying to issue an outstanding warrant on Jack.

On patrol one afternoon, Leach spotted Joe at a stoplight and pulled him over, hoping to get some information on Jack's whereabouts. It so happened that Leach knew Jack and Joe well enough to tell the two apart, even from a distance.

After Leach had stepped out of his car to speak to Joe, he happened to spot Jack nearby, walking across the street. Although Leach and Jack made eye contact, Jack just kept on walking as though nothing was wrong. Time for a little reverse psychology.

"I was on to their little game of mistaken identities, so I thought I'd give them a taste of their own medicine," Leach remembers. "I knew if I called out his real name, Jack would start running. So I didn't. Instead, I called out the name of his brother—who was standing beside me.

" 'Hey, Joe!' I yelled. 'Come over here and talk to me, would ya?' "

Now Jack, fooled into thinking that Officer Leach thought *he* was Joe, walked right up to Leach, who then grabbed the real jerk, er, Jack, by the shirt.

"You're under arrest, *Jack*," Leach said.

"Hey . . . but I thought that you thought . . . that I was. . . . Damn! Man, that's not right."

Jack knew he'd been had, and he didn't like it one bit. He had fallen for his own game.

It Never Dawned on Him 5

The Las Vegas dawn sky was gray and the first rays of sunlight were peeking over the desert mountains. Officer Gordon Martines was routinely working the red-eye shift when a car roared past him at sixty-five miles per hour in a thirty-five zone. Martines took off in hot pursuit.

After he had pulled his lead-footed prey off to the side of the road, Officer Martines exited his car. The man stepped out of his and walked toward Martines in an obvious state of nervousness, gazing toward the desert and the brightening horizon.

"I know you're not going to believe me," he told Martines, "but I'm a vampire, and I've got to get back to my coffin before the sun comes up!"

"Okay," Martines said, a brow arched. "I'll write this real quick so you can get going."

The guy was back in his car and out of sight before the sun appeared, so Officer Martines never saw if the man really was a vampire . . . or just plain batty.

As Innocent as a Baby

Retired police captain Don Parker of Pensacola, Florida, knows as well as anyone that mistakes are sometimes made when it comes to enforcing the law. That appeared to be the case in an apparent shoplifting incident. When the policeman arrived on the scene at the security office of a large department store, he saw a young mother with an infant in a stroller. The woman was crying her eyes out as two store security people looked on.

"But I keep telling you, I didn't do nothing," she wailed as tears streamed down her cheeks.

The police officer asked the head of store security to step outside to discuss the case in private. The woman was suspected of stealing several gold chains, but no evidence had been uncovered during a search of the woman and the diaper bag. "I know she's got them someplace," the security guard muttered. "I just have to find them."

Back inside, the woman was still weeping. "I ain't got

Suddenly, his hand went down into his diaper and came out clutching three gold chains.

nothing to hide," she said tearfully. "I just want to take my baby and go home." The baby was starting to whimper, and the woman bent down to kiss him. "Now don't you fuss, darlin'. We'll be going home soon."

She began repacking the diaper bag as the baby continued to whine, plucking at his diaper and squirming in the stroller. Suddenly, his hand went down into his diaper and came out clutching three gold chains. He flung them onto the floor and went back for more.

By the time it was over, nine expensive gold chains had been recovered. The mother watched in grim-faced silence as the chains were gathered up, but as soon as the officer started reading her Miranda rights to her, she exploded.

"I hope you're not thinking about arresting me," she spat out. The officer replied that this was exactly what he had in mind. She shook her head and pointed at the infant. "He's the one who stole the chains," she said huffily. "I didn't do anything!"

Roll Call for Criminals

Getting a sincere confession of guilt that is admissible in court is often difficult, but when it happens, the sense of satisfaction makes up for all the lean times.

One such case in the Southwest involved two men on trial for armed robbery and assault. You could hear a pin drop in the courtroom as the prosecutor questioned the victim, who, along with her husband, had been robbed at gunpoint. Her voice quavered, and she seemed terribly frightened. Noting this, the prosecutor raised his voice and turned his gaze away from the woman, hoping not to intimidate her any further.

"Are the two men who committed this horrible crime in the courtroom today?" he sternly asked.

At that, the two defendants raised their hands. The courtroom gallery and even the judge snickered. Noticing the two arms in the air, the prosecutor said, "Your honor, may the record show that the defendants raised their hands and have just confessed to the crime."

The Not-So Good Samaritans

One chilly winter night in Birmingham, Alabama, officer Anthony Parks received a call that an apartment burglary was in progress. When Parks got there, the residents greeted him and explained that they had the burglar in custody. Sure enough, the culprit was sitting at the kitchen table finishing off a hamburger. This deserved an explanation.

It seems that our apartment residents had made a burger run to a nearby drive-through. When they returned, they noticed that their apartment door had been jimmied and was partially open. They immediately called 911 and then surprised the crook going through their closets. He tried to explain:

"Well, it was so cold out there tonight, and I don't have any place to stay. So I broke in just to get warm and maybe take a warmer jacket for the long, cold night ahead."

The burglar's sob story touched the apartment

dwellers' hearts. So they shared their burgers with the burglar and gave him a denim jacket. The victims actually pleaded with Parks to not arrest their unfortunate burglar. But the law is the law, and this chilly willy had broken it, so it was off to the booking room.

"We always pat down and search the prisoners when they're being booked, and that's what I was doing to this poor man when I made an amazing discovery," Parks said. "He was in possession of a quantity of crack cocaine. And this was as much a surprise to him as it was to me, because I found it in the pocket of the denim jacket that his victims had just given him. Possession is still nine-tenths of the law, so I had to book him for possession of cocaine. But at least he spent the night in a warm jail cell."

Every good deed deserves another, so the Birmingham police paid a return visit to the not-so-good Samaritans who were themselves booked after a search of the apartment turned up drugs and drug paraphernalia.

Parlez-vous Français?

The small town of Phoenix in upstate New York is only ninety miles from the Canadian border, and occasional language problems crop up with the French-speaking neighbors to the north.

Deputy Bill Cromie was on routine patrol one evening when a big Cadillac with Ontario plates zipped by. He stopped the car and asked the driver for his license. Speaking in French, the man indicated that he didn't understand. Cromie made some hand signals to indicate he wanted the man's driver's license, but the driver just shook his head.

"Right from the start, I had the idea that he understood a lot more than he was admitting," Cromie says. "After all, even in Canada, the first thing a cop is going to ask for during a traffic stop is the driver's license."

Cromie attempted to explain that he was going to write the man a ticket for speeding and that he would have to make an immediate appearance before the judge. The guy shook his head the entire time, and Cromie was beginning to get irritated at what he was convinced was nothing more than a charade.

"Sir, do you know what a *bastille* is?" Cromie finally asked.

"You give me ticket?" the man said, finally breaking his silence in barely understandable English.

"Oh, it will be much better than that," Cromie said. "You're going to get to meet our judge."

"I no understand."

Nevertheless, the man was soon standing in front of the judge, who read the charges to him—in English. The guy shrugged helplessly and in fractured English indicated that he didn't understand. Looking as pitiful as he could make himself look, the driver rattled off a long response in French. The judge waited until he finished, nodded politely, and in perfect French repeated the charges. Then he informed him—again in French—that the fine would be a hundred dollars.

"A hundred dollars!" the driver yelped in clear and understandable English. Realizing his error, he quickly reverted to his garbled speech again, but it was too late.

"Yes, the fine will be a hundred dollars," the bilingual judge repeated with a smile, "U.S. currency only."

Bad Excuse No. 53

Most folks probably have been stopped for speeding at one time or another and are usually ready with a perfectly good excuse for breaking the law. Sgt. Johnny Cooley of Birmingham, Alabama, has worked traffic on the local interstate highway for almost a quarter of a century, but the creative excuses he hears never cease to amaze him—as was the case with the following, which occurred just as rush-hour traffic on a Friday afternoon was starting to hit full stride.

Sergeant Cooley popped on his radar gun and sat back in his cruiser. It was a beautiful afternoon. Maybe this would be one afternoon rush hour that would just roll on smoothly like the swiftly setting sun. No such luck.

Within moments, Cooley's radar gun screamed. When he checked the speed, the gun read "102." That's one hundred two miles per hour in a fifty-five-mile-per-hour speed zone! The car blew by in the left lane, and Cooley peeled out behind with lights and siren on. Three miles down the road, he had the speeder pulled off to the shoulder.

"I always ask the motorists first why they were speeding, because you never know when someone's in the middle of a real emergency and might need help," Cooley says. "The last thing I want to do is impede someone who has a legitimate medical emergency. So I asked him if he had a problem."

The driver was very calm and almost sheepish when he answered Cooley, "Uh, no . . . no, sir."

"So I asked him why he was going one hundred two miles per hour in a fifty-five speed zone."

"Well, I just got my car washed and I . . . uh . . . well, I was trying to blow-dry it," the guy said.

Cooley asked him how much the car wash had cost him. The driver looked confused but told the officer "five bucks."

"So I handed him the ticket and told him the blow-dry was going to cost him one hundred twenty-five dollars."

Paging All Dumb Crooks

Officer Aaron Graham is the media information officer for the Louisville (Kentucky) Police Department. His job is to issue press releases regarding his department's arrests, investigations, personnel changes, and events, and he tries to answer any questions the media might have. Sometimes the hardened reporters who cover headquarters and review the police blotter have a hard time believing Graham's press releases. But occasionally the truth about dumb criminals defies even Officer Graham's imagination.

Graham recounted for us in detail the story of an officer in his department who got a call saying there had been a house break-in and that several items were missing from the house. So he responded and, well, it gets pretty unbelievable from there on.

The officer was taking down a laundry list of items stolen along with descriptions, serial numbers, and values when the owner of the house noticed that his son's beeper had been taken. Just on a lark, the officer called the beeper number. Within moments, the thief was calling the house that he had just robbed an hour and a half earlier. The owner of the house also had caller I.D. on his telephone, so now the thief's name and phone number were scrolling across the little LCD screen. The owner kept him in conversation.

"No, I didn't beep you. It must've been my son, and he's in the shower. Are you at home?"

"Yes, sir."

"Well, could you try back in about five minutes? He should be out by then."

"Okay."

Five minutes later, true to his word, he called back. By this time the officers had discovered where he lived— just a few blocks away. The victim was still talking to the robber on the phone when the police burst into the robber's house and apprehended him with the stolen beeper in his hand.

"Paging Mr. Knucklehead. Mr. Knucklehead, you have a call . . ."

Collar around the Ring

One jewel thief learned the hard way that diamonds aren't *really* forever. Providence, Rhode Island, police chief William Devine explains:

"The suspect wasn't really a jewel thief. He was really just a shoplifter who bit off a little more than he could chew," Devine said.

It seems our two-bit thief had gone into a jewelry store and asked to see some diamond rings. The clerk obliged him and brought out a tray of the store's largest, most expensive pieces. Our would-be jewel thief tried on just about every ring in the place but just couldn't find the right one. He was about to give up and leave when the clerk noticed that one of the rings, the most expensive one, was missing. Naturally, the clerk mentioned this.

The thief was outraged at what obviously was an accusation directed at him. He denied any knowledge of the ring and accused the clerk of trying to pull a fast one. The clerk called the police anyway and, just before the

Just before the cops arrived, she noticed her "customer" pop something into his mouth.

cops arrived, she noticed her "customer" pop something into his mouth.

The police had a good idea that the man was in possession of the stolen ring, but they couldn't find it on him. Maybe it was *in* him. So they decided to search the suspect internally.

Sure enough, an x ray of the suspect's abdomen showed a ring cuddling up against the ham sandwich he had eaten for lunch an hour earlier. But before the jewelry store owner could positively identify the ring, everyone had to wait for nature to take its course.

Like sands through the hourglass, the ring did materialize in due time. And, yes, it was the stolen one. The man was booked and convicted.

We just had to ask about the method of evidence retrieval used by the police in this case. But all Chief Devine would say about it was, "That job went to the officer who was low man on the totem pole."

How well do you know the dumb criminal mind?

Suppose that you and two dumb criminal friends have just escaped from an American prison near the Mexican border. You swim across the Rio Grande River, and you're safely into Mexico when you realize that your pickup man hasn't shown up yet. Do you and your friends . . .

a) **Swim back across the Rio Grande into the States to find a phone and get arrested by the state police?**
b) **Split up and go your own separate ways?**
c) **Find a place to hide and wait for him?**

HINT: Remember. You're not just criminals, you're dumb criminals.

Of course, the answer could only be (a). Believe it or not, that was the choice that the real three amigos made!

13 Ant That a Shame?

Capt. Arnetta Nunn of Birmingham, Alabama, got a "disturbing the peace" call in her rookie days that turned out to be somewhat odd. She rolled on the call, but when she arrived at the address, she couldn't hear anything unusual. No deafening music. No loud voices. No noise. Nothing. She was about to call back the person who had made the complaint, when two men ran out of the house and hotfooted it through the yard.

"Law-abiding citizens don't run from the police, so my partner and I pursued the two males on foot," Nunn says. "My partner grabbed one of them almost immediately, but my guy was a little faster. He turned a corner and darted behind a neighbor's house just a few feet ahead of me. When I came around the corner, he had disappeared. I looked everywhere, but the guy had just vaporized."

Nunn prided herself on her running speed, and she just couldn't believe she had lost this guy. Then she noticed that the bushes up against the house were shaking, just a little at first, but then more violently. She pointed her gun at the bushes.

"All right, come on out with your hands in the air!" she yelled.

Sure enough, the culprit stepped out, but he couldn't keep his hands in the air. He would scratch his back and chest frantically and then put them into the air again.

"It seems the man had lain down right in a nest of fire ants, and they were eating him alive. It's a good thing. I might never have found him if the ants hadn't helped out."

Sorry about That

Officer Dan Newman of the Las Vegas (Nevada) Police Department told America's Dumbest Criminals of an unintentionally funny event that occurred while he was involved in a routine narcotics operation.

"We raided the house of a known drug dealer, and the suspect, upon our entering, went running down a hallway toward the back of the home," Newman said. "Unbeknownst to us, the man was an amputee who usually wore a prosthesis. After a moment or two of hide-and-seek, my partner yelled out from the back of the house, 'Hey, I've got the suspect here in the back bedroom . . . and he's unarmed!' "

It wasn't until Newman and his partner entered the room and saw the prosthetic limb lying on the bed that they realized the true impact of the statement. Even the suspect laughed—but not for long. He was arrested for possession of a controlled substance with the intent of resale.

Robbery Returns

Investigator Lonnie Isom of Pensacola, Florida, had his case wrapped up in record time. Suspect, evidence, victim, and stolen goods were all coming together beautifully at the crime scene. It was almost like the ending of a Charlie Chan movie. And Officer Isom had made only two trips to the scene of the crime: first to take down the victim's report and a second time to nab the suspect with the goods.

On his first visit to the shopping center parking lot, a woman had reported to him that someone had broken into her car and stolen some merchandise that she had just purchased at an electronics store. This is an all-too-common call, and the clues were few to none, but Isom made as detailed a report as possible and began to check on other thefts in the area and links to the usual suspects.

He needn't have bothered. Less than twenty-four hours later, the woman called back and asked Isom to come quickly to the electronics store. He arrived to find her holding a suspect, assisted by an off-duty deputy and a clerk.

It seems that the woman had returned to the store to find out the exact value of the items for her insurance claim. While she was trying to describe what she had bought, a man came in to ask for a refund on several items.

"I had one like that! And that! Wait, those are mine!" she cried.

The thief was trying to return her stolen things right in front of her!

Isom, in his best Perry Mason-Charlie Chan investigative style, laid out the crime when he arrived. "*You* stole *these* items which *she* purchased at *this* store. *You* took them from *her* car in *that* parking lot and were trying to return them for money at the *same* store while *she* was trying to determine their value."

Everything sure seemed to jibe, and there was no way to deny the obvious, so the suspect didn't try. But later that night, when Isom was questioning him at the jail, the thief with the bad timing complained that someone had stolen his soap and towel from his cell.

The Fall to Grace

16

Sgt. Johnny Cooley was running radar on the interstate outside Birmingham, Alabama, one night when he witnessed a bona fide traffic miracle.

The street was slick from a rain that had just ended, and the pace of traffic was again picking up. An eighteen-wheeler came barreling around a curve, when a car suddenly switched lanes directly into the truck's path. The truck driver hit the brakes and began to hydroplane across the lanes, out of control. The cab of the truck hit the railing at full speed and the trailer followed, disappearing over the edge of an overpass.

Cooley knew there was a basketball court below, and chances were real good that a pickup game was in progress. Cooley quickly radioed in for paramedics and backup. When he got to the twisted, crushed semi, his worst fears surfaced, although it appeared that the basketball players had escaped: they were all busy looting the trailer of its beer and wine haul. When they saw Cooley, they made a fast break toward the shadows.

Sergeant Cooley sighed as he stepped out of his cruiser for the worst part of his job—visually confirming the traffic fatality. He stepped up on what was left of the cab's running board and peered into a small opening that used to be the driver's side window. He gritted his teeth and swallowed hard. But when he looked in, he couldn't believe his eyes. There was a woman lying comfortably stretched out on the seat, reading a book.

"Ma'am? Are you okay?"

The woman calmly closed her book and smiled, "Oh, I'm fine, thank you."

Cooley could not believe that she had survived the crash, much less the sixty-five-foot drop.

"Were you driving the rig, ma'am?"

She smiled again, "Yes, sir, but I had some help."

"Help? You mean another driver? Where is he? The paramedics are here."

"My copilot's right here," she said, holding up the Bible she had been reading. "God."

Granted, the only dummies in this story were the freeloading basketballers, but it's a story that just had to be told.

Not Quite Clever Enough

A young man in Pensacola, Florida, was enterprising enough to "acquire" a woman's purse.

He was also clever enough to forge the woman's signature on a note saying: "It's my son's birthday, and I am too sick to get out of bed. Please let my son spend up to five hundred dollars. Thanks very much."

Our young entrepreneur went to a department store and purchased a lot of nice clothes and some really cool shoes. He signed the charge slip, gave the lady his *real* home phone number, and went merrily on his way.

The police were having a nice chat with his *real* mom by the time he got his packages home.

Be Careful How You Choose Your Friends

Dumb criminals come in all shapes and sizes as well as personality types. Some are quiet, some are shy, some are talkative, and some are downright friendly. When Bill Page was an Illinois state trooper, he ran into one of the friendly ones. Not necessarily smart, but definitely friendly.

It all happened during a long and boring midnight shift in a small rural Illinois county. Around four in the morning, Page stopped at a local restaurant for breakfast. He sat with a couple of deputy acquaintances, and as they were talking they saw a pickup truck pull into the parking lot. The driver got out, and all three lawmen recognized him immediately. He was a local thief named Jim who had been in and out of trouble most of his life.

The man walked into the restaurant, spotted the three cops, and came over to chat. They talked for a few minutes, and Jim finally walked off. Looking at the truck through the window of the restaurant, the three diners noticed that it had a company logo painted on the door. One of the deputies called the manager of the company who owned the truck and asked him if Jim was one of the company's employees. The manager said he certainly was not, since his company was not in the habit of hiring known thieves.

Poor Jim was taken into custody before he had a chance to eat his breakfast. By the time the men arrived at the sheriff's office, the company's manager had called back to tell them the company office had been burglarized and the truck stolen. They cleared the case and recovered the stolen truck, although Trooper Page still wonders why Jim would be so stupid as to stop at a restaurant where three marked police cars were parked.

If at First You Don't Succeed . . .

Perseverance and determination are frequently the marks of successful people. But we emphasize *frequently,* meaning *not always.* Former Baltimore, Maryland, police officer Frank Walmer remembers a determined burglar who persevered until he managed to get himself arrested.

Walmer and his partner were dispatched to a burglary in progress in a residential neighborhood. "We arrived and contacted the woman who had called," Walmer said. "She told us that someone had been trying to break through her basement door and that he was still at it. As we stood in the living room, we could plainly hear all sorts of thumping and bumping coming from the basement."

The woman led the two officers down the stairs and showed them the door in question.

"It was just as she described," Walmer said. "Someone was on the other side of the door, methodically kicking

He twisted and wiggled and, with a great deal of effort, finally
managed to squeeze through the hole he had made.

it in. The bottom panel was beginning to give way. In a moment or two a hand reached through, but the hole wasn't big enough yet."

More kicking gradually widened the hole while the officers looked on. When the opening was large enough, a head popped through.

"My partner and I were standing on either side of the door," Walmer says, "but the guy never looked around. He twisted and wiggled and, with a great deal of effort, finally managed to squeeze through the hole he had made. Breathing hard, he stood up, dusted himself off, and suddenly realized he was looking down two gun barrels.

"At that point," says Officer Walmer, "we felt we had a pretty strong case."

Mental Blocks

Responding to a burglary call in Birmingham, Alabama, Lieutenant Jay Macintosh arrived at the scene to find the would-be burglars lying, exhausted, in back of the building. Too tired to do anything but talk, they explained that they had come equipped with picks and sledgehammers to pound away at the thick brick wall.

When they finally broke through the bricks some forty-five minutes later, they were stunned at what they found. It seems that the building owners, in order to prevent flooding, had built up the back of the property and erected a retaining wall. It was this wall, not the wall of the actual store, that the burglars had worked so hard to breach. Once they were through, our stonebreakers found themselves not inside the building, but on the roof!

Ever heard the phrase "thick as a brick"? At any rate, these guys got some good practice for a future occupation: breaking rocks in a prison camp.

21 The (Ex)-Terminator

Sgt. Perry Knowles got a call one night announcing that shots were being fired at one of the juke joints in Pensacola, Florida. Knowles was only moments from the little tavern, so he responded immediately and sped to the scene.

A few moments after arriving, he realized he was the first on the scene and that the shots were still ringing out. They seemed to be coming from inside. Knowles drew his gun and cautiously approached the front door. Inside, people were still dancing and shooting pool as though nothing out of the ordinary was going on. Another shot rang out. Without waiting for backup, Knowles dashed in, just as another shot sounded from the back of the club.

Gun drawn, Knowles hurried down a hallway and then crept around the corner, where he saw a man facing the other way with a pistol in hand, following the path of a huge cockroach. *Blam!* He blasted the cockroach with a close-range shot from a .38 and blew a big hole in

Blam! **He blasted the cockroach with a close-range shot from a
.38 and blew a big hole in the wall.**

the wall. After two more direct hits, the (ex)terminator broke open his cylinder to reload. That's when Sergeant Knowles jumped out from behind the corner.

"What in the world are you doing?" Knowles yelled while disarming the man.

"Shooting cockroaches!" the shooter said, apparently seeing nothing odd about his answer.

"Why?" Knowles asked.

"Well, we've tried everything else, and nothing has worked."

In Your Face

Police captain Mike Coppage of Birmingham, Alabama, remembers the time that one of his fellow officers was on his way home in a marked unit and had just stopped by Shoney's, a restaurant known for its strawberry pies. He picked up a whole pie to go and was just about to leave the parking lot when a call came through from the dispatcher. A break-in had just occurred in a small business right behind the restaurant.

Leaving his patrol unit behind in the restaurant parking lot, the officer walked around to the crime scene and began his investigation. While he was dusting for prints, the officer suddenly heard a desperate cry for help on his walkie-talkie.

"Help! Help!" cried the voice. "I'm in trouble. Help me!"

The call was coming from a police radio. It was an officer in trouble!

In response, the police dispatcher desperately tried to

pinpoint the distressed officer's location: "Where are you? What is your location?"

"I don't know!" came the response. "Just send help."

"What is your patrol car number?" the dispatcher asked.

"I don't know."

Realizing now that it had to be a civilian on the police mike, and believing that the officer was too severely injured to respond, the dispatcher put out the call: "All units, officer down!"

"Sir," the dispatcher then said to the voice on the radio, "I need the number of the unit."

"Okay. I see it now. It's 412. Car 412."

By this time, our crime-scene officer was running back to his car at top speed when it dawned on him—car 412 was *his* unit. He raced back to his police cruiser, and there stood the man, still clutching the microphone. His face, neck, and the front of his shirt were covered with what had to be blood. He was breathing sporadically and obviously in a state of shock and confusion. The officer tried to calm the man down and was about to administer first aid when he noticed that the "blood" on his hands was thick and sticky. The man was covered with strawberry pie!

Wait a minute, thought the officer, *I just bought a . . . oh, man, don't tell me that. Noooo.* By now the cop was peering into his patrol car. It looked like an octopus had had a strawberry and whipped cream food fight in the backseat.

The "injured" man, a street person—and drunk out of his mind—had walked by and seen the pie in the cruiser's backseat. He had then crawled inside the squad car and helped himself to that strawberry pie without benefit of utensils. For some unknown reason, he had completely freaked out and called for help after eating the entire pie with his face.

"We laugh about it now," Captain Coppage says, "but at the time the officer was so mad he couldn't see straight."

23 Bedrock Blues

Sgt. Chip Simmons works undercover narcotics in a medium-sized city in the South. Like almost every other city in the United States, this particular city was known for having a few hot spots for drugs. The cops would do a sweep of those hot spots every few weeks or so, then the traffickers would get released and move a few blocks away to resume business. It was an ongoing cycle.

Sergeant Simmons was frustrated by this slow repetition of arrest, release, move on, and start up again. So he and his fellow officers would try to keep the trade in total chaos by staging frequent, sudden, and very visible "jump outs." Five or six plainclothes officers with badges and guns would target a hot spot for the evening, usually a nightclub parking lot, and, literally, jump out of an unmarked van to surprise the drug traffickers.

In the wee hours of a chilly morning, just about a half-

284

hour before the legal closing time for taverns, Simmons and the van of officers eased in quietly to a space in a parking lot where twelve dealers were doing business. The dealers were already moving toward the van to sell dope to the new arrival when the back doors popped open and the Trojan van spewed out its load of narcotics officers. Dealers scattered, some falling to the pavement, some disappearing into the night, most finally surrendering.

Simmons collared one individual who was in possession of several "rocks" of crack cocaine but who didn't have any identification on him.

"What's your name?" Simmons asked.

"Tommy."

"Tommy what?"

"Tommy Smith, but most people call me Tiger."

"Tommy 'Tiger' Smith?"

"No, Thomas L. Smith."

The name games continued, and the officer got the distinct impression that this suspect was lying. Chip Simmons was the wrong man to choose for verbal sparring.

"Where do you live, Tiger?"

"Johnson Avenue," Tiger smugly replied.

"What number on Johnson Avenue?" Simmons asked, laying the bait.

"100 Johnson Avenue."

"The blue house?"

"Yeah, big blue house."

"And there's always a green car in the driveway?"

"That's my green car."

Simmons grinned from ear to ear. "Now I know you're lying."

Tiger was indignant. "I am not."

"I know you're lying, because I know who lives in that blue house. And it's not you; it's the Rubbles!"

Tiger's face went slack. He went back to rule number one of dumb crime: Deny, deny, deny!

"They do not!"

All the officers were now breaking into laughter as Simmons closed in for the kill.

"Yes, they do! Betty and Barney Rubble, good friends of mine, known 'em for years. They've always lived at 100 Johnson Avenue!"

Tiger was in a corner, but then a light went off in his empty little head.

"They don't live there now . . . because I bought the house from the Rubbles last month. That's who I bought the house from . . . the Rubbles! Betty and Barney!"

Later that night, Tiger's fingerprints revealed the dealer's real name. And guess what: it wasn't Fred Flintstone!

I Should Have Made That to Go

Sgt. Larry McDonald was called to a break-in at a Birmingham, Alabama, grade school one night. Upon arriving, he was met by another officer. While the backup unit staked out the front of the school, Officer McDonald walked around back and began looking through windows to see if the burglar might still be inside.

While walking past the cafeteria window, McDonald saw the intruder sitting at one of the lunchroom tables with a big hunk of ham in front of him. The burglar also had in front of him some mustard, bread, and a bag of potato chips. He was making himself a midnight snack. Problem was, it wasn't his food. Or his house.

"About the time I put my light on him, the officer in front had gained entrance to the school, so we placed the man under arrest and took him into custody," McDonald says. "He should have made that sandwich to go."

Debriefing

Bank robbing is one of those high-pressure professions. Stress certainly is part of the job—and one, we presume, that is not covered in the group medical plan.

Not all bank robbers are up to the task. Take the case of the Charlotte, North Carolina, bank robber, fleeing from the scene of his crime. In a brilliant flash of inspiration, he stripped to his underwear, figuring there was no way he could be identified by specific articles of clothing. Next, of course, he would stuff the large bundle of heisted greenbacks down the front of his underwear.

His plan seemingly worked. No one came forward to identify the robber. Someone, however, *did* call the police and point him out as the "sweaty man wearing nothing but strangely bulging underwear." The officers report that after the man was "debriefed," the money was recovered.

This Guy Is Falling

26

Birmingham, Alabama, officer Ken McGinnis knows that there are times when serving an arrest warrant is anything but routine. There's always the chance that whoever is being arrested won't come without some show of force. But this was one arrest that made up for what it lacked in real danger with a few good belly laughs.

While serving the warrant, McGinnis and his partner stood at the door of the man's house and knocked several times, but no one answered, although they could hear movement inside. Finally, a woman answered the door and listened as the two officers explained why they were there. When they were finished, the woman said that she was the man's mother and hadn't seen her son in several days.

"Do you mind if we take a look inside, ma'am?" McGinnis asked.

"Not at all," she said. "Come on in and look around."

The two officers entered the house and started down the hallway with the mother right behind them. "Lord knows where that boy is," she was saying.

Then, abruptly, they heard a sharp cracking sound overhead, followed by a shower of plaster and a falling body. Their suspect hit the floor right in front of them. He did a belly flop and must have bounced two feet. Then he lay still, the wind knocked out of him.

After allowing the man time to catch his breath and brush off some of the plaster, McGinnis and his partner rolled the guy over and handcuffed him. "Guess the Lord *did* know where he was," McGinnis remembers. "And it was sure good of Him to pass along the information."

Unlucky Numbers

27

Officer Dennis Shepard was on routine patrol late one Friday night in the charming little town of Franklin, Tennessee, when he and his partner noticed a man scurrying along one of the main streets of town. The pedestrian appeared to be quite nervous and was clutching something in his hand while continually looking back over his shoulder. He also appeared to be trying to stay in the shadows, avoiding the street lamps.

As the officers' car approached him, the man's face lit up into a broad smile, and he began motioning frantically for them to pull over. Officer Shepard recognized him now. He was the man known locally as Pot Pie, a harmless individual who, over the years, had occasionally been arrested for public intoxication.

"Boy, am I glad to see you guys," Pot Pie blurted out. "I need a ride home, officers. This has been my lucky day!"

"Your lucky day?" they asked curiously. "How so?"

"I've been playin' the numbers for ten years, and today my ship came in. Looky here."

They looked at the bundle the man was waving in the air.

"What is it?" they asked.

"What it is," he said with pride, "is the seven hundred fifty dollars cash that I won today after all these years."

"You won this money gambling on the numbers?" the officer asked, hoping that it might dawn on Pot Pie what he was telling the police about his own illegal activity.

"I sure did," he answered with an even bigger grin. "Ten years, and I finally won. Seven hundred fifty dollars! Hot damn! I been out celebratin', and now I need a ride home to make sure nobody takes it away from me."

Shepard shook his head sadly. *Why didn't this guy just call a cab?* he thought. This was one of those times that he wished he didn't have to do what he was about to do.

"You sure you won that money playin' the numbers, Pot Pie?" he asked, still trying to find an out for the guy.

"Oh, yeah," he said. "I played the numbers all right, and here's the money to prove it."

The officers looked at each other. Pot Pie was as happy as could be. His grin reminded Shepard of one of those smiley-face buttons, and he hated being the one to paint on the big red circle with the slash through it.

"I'm afraid, then, that we're going to have to arrest you," he told Pot Pie.

"Arrest me? For what?"

"Don't you know that it's against the law to gamble on the numbers in Tennessee?"

"Sure, I do . . . but I won! I . . ." Then reality slowly set in. His face sank. "What about the money?" he asked.

"Well, I'm afraid we're going to have to confiscate the money as evidence."

Pot Pie's face sank even lower. "I was so happy winnin' that money that I plumb forgot that the numbers was against the law. Man, I should've called a cab!"

Actually, things didn't turn out so badly for our dumb criminal. When Pot Pie went to court, the judge took pity on him. He fined him court costs only and returned nearly five hundred dollars to him.

The Honeymoon's Over

Police officer Mary Wiley was used to working undercover. She had been involved in more than a hundred prostitution stings in and around Birmingham, Alabama. So she pretty much assumed she had seen it all—until she met the man in the tuxedo.

When working a sting, Officer Wiley would pose as a streetwalker while other officers monitored, from down the street, her conversations with potential clients. Once a deal was struck with a "john," or client, she would direct him to meet her around the corner, where he would promptly be arrested for solicitation. If he was married, the first question out of his mouth was likely to be, "Will my wife find out about this?"

That's more or less what happened with the tuxedo-clad gentleman. He pulled his car up to the curb, rolled down the window, stuck his elegantly groomed head out the window, and propositioned her. Wiley did her job, and it wasn't until after the tuxedoed man had been

Believe it or not, the man had taken his wedding vows only four hours earlier.

arrested that she found out why he was dressed so nicely. It was his wedding day!

Believe it or not, the man had taken his wedding vows only four hours earlier. He'd left the reception, still dressed to the nines, to buy more beer, and he then apparently decided to stop for one more purchase.

"Is my wife going to find out?" he asked.

"I wouldn't worry too much about that," Wiley responded. "If she does find out, you probably won't have a wife anymore."

At the very least, we'd bet she threw a lot more than rice at him when he returned to the reception.

Yeah, and One Size Fits All!

Officer Max Kent was driving down the road on a balmy Florida evening, minding his own business, when a small car accelerated away from an intersection, spinning its tires for about twenty feet—"laying a patch," if you will.

Just another routine traffic stop, right? In this book? No way.

The small red car picked up speed as Kent hit his lights and siren. But almost as quickly as he floored it, the speeding driver began to brake and pull over. It would seem the driver had second thoughts about trying to run from the law.

Officer Kent approached the driver's side and began to question the man.

"Sir, could I see your driver's—"

Suddenly, the red car peeled out at full speed, spitting gravel and dust inches away from Kent's nose and toes.

The officer leaped back into his squad car and again gave chase as he called in for backup.

Again, the man pulled over within moments. This time Officer Kent drew his pistol as he approached the window.

The man was already waving his hands and screaming, "I'm sorry! I'm sorry! My foot slipped off the clutch, and I had the dang thing in gear."

Before Officer Kent got a chance to tell the gentleman what he thought of that story, the car scrubbed out one more time. This time Ol' Slippery Foot "slipped" down a residential side street that just happened to be a dead end. Officer Kent radioed in his position and jumped out of his car in a firing position. His gun was trained on the red car, now stopped in the cul-de-sac. He could just hear the man saying, "I'm sorry" again.

Then—you guessed it—his foot "slipped" once more. Only this time the red car was accelerating straight at Kent. He was ready to disable the vehicle or the driver or both when the car suddenly came to a halt about twenty feet away from Kent and his cruiser.

Needless to say, Kent got the suspect out of the car, cuffed him, and pulled him onto the pavement before his foot had another chance to "slip."

Gotta Match?

Capt. Mike Coppage, one of our Birmingham, Alabama, police acquaintances, told America's Dumbest Criminals of a strange domestic violence call that came in from a frantic woman. It seems she and her husband had been having quite a bit of trouble lately, and things had escalated to the point that her husband was now threatening to kill himself and her.

Police units and a S.W.A.T. team were immediately dispatched to the address, where they heard shouts and threats coming from inside the house. "I'll do it! Don't think I won't . . . 'cause I will. I'll kill myself!" Obviously, things were really getting out of control in there. When the police negotiator got the man on the phone, Coppage's crew realized just how bad it was.

"I'm gonna kill myself, the man threatened. "I've doused myself and the house with gasoline, and I'm gonna set myself on fire right now."

"Hey, we can work this out, Ronnie," the negotiator told him. "Come on outside. Let's talk about it."

"There ain't nothin' left to talk about, man. It's over."

Then the man set the phone down. There was an eerie silence.

Captain Coppage looked at the negotiator. He nodded his head. It was time to send in the S.W.A.T. team. The captain was about to give the signal to storm the house when suddenly the man was back on the line.

"Hey, y'all still there?" the man asked.

"Yeah, we're here."

"You got any matches?"

"Matches? You want matches?"

"Yeah, matches. You know, the kind you light? I can't find any in here."

"Let me look," the quick-thinking negotiator told him. "Yeah, I've got a book of 'em right here, Ronnie, but you're going to have to come out here and get them. I can't come in there."

"All right," Ronnie said. "I'll be right out."

True to his word, the man walked outside, where he was quickly apprehended.

Reach out and Touch Someone

31

Wanted for several dozen burglaries, East Coast fugitive Lester Willet had been eluding capture for several weeks. Although he had been seen in various bars, he always managed to be gone by the time the cops arrived. Friendly and outgoing, he had plenty of friends quick to tip him off each time the long arm of the law reached out to snag him.

But Lester Willet had a weakness, and her name was Charlene. A cocktail waitress at Taylor's Place, Charlene was a heavily made-up, gum-chewing, buxom beauty. Sadly, Willet's was an unrequited love, because Charlene adamantly refused to go out with him.

The investigator pursuing Willet learned about his infatuation with Charlene from one of his informants. He further learned that Charlene had this particular night off and that Willet had been calling her steadily from

Taylor's pay phone, trying to talk her into going out with him.

Seized by a sudden flash of inspiration, the investigator decided to have someone call Taylor's, impersonate Charlene's voice, and ask to speak to Willet. Once Willet got on the phone, it would be a simple matter to swoop down and capture him. It was a good idea, although finding a convincing female voice was going to be difficult. Then someone suggested Dan Bulger.

Bulger was a brash communications dispatcher who also happened to be a wonderful mimic. He was on duty at the time, so the investigator sought him out and explained the plan. The capture team would wait a block or so from Taylor's as Dan, using his best female voice, called the bar, identified himself as Charlene, and asked for Willet. When Willet picked up the phone, the team would be notified by one of the other dispatchers and then make their move.

Their scheme worked perfectly. The pay phone was close to the main door, and when the team came around the corner there was Willet, the phone jammed against one ear and his hand pressed against the other. "Baby, you know I'm crazy about you!" he yelled into the phone. "You go out with me and you won't regret it, I promise."

So intent was he on the conversation that he didn't

notice he was now surrounded by uniforms. He had a big smile on his face and was nodding his head. "Room nineteen at the Sunset Motel. Right."

The investigator stepped forward and tapped him on the shoulder. Willet looked up, and the smile disappeared. "Uh, I got to go, baby," he said. He hung up and shook his head. "Well, I hope you guys are happy. I was fixing to meet one of the finest-looking women I have ever seen, and she was even going to pay for the room."

It was just a short trip back to the jail, but Willet complained about his bad luck the whole way. Just to rub it in, the investigator had Dan come over from the radio room. Willet was being fingerprinted when Dan stepped to the door and, using his Charlene voice, said, "Honey, I told you to meet me at the Sunset Motel."

Willet spun around so fast he almost knocked over the fingerprint stand. Dan gave him a big smile. "But I've changed my mind, sugar. You pay for the room."

32 Color Me Dumb

Officers Robert Cox and Ed Leach of Birmingham, Alabama, were on patrol in an area known for its drug houses when they spotted five men, most of them familiar looking, in an old Datsun with expired tags. The car also had two different-colored fenders and was brown on one side and white on the other. The officers shook their heads over that eye-catching repair job while they issued the driver a ticket for the expired tags.

About three hours later, the police department received a call that a robbery had gone down at a convenience store. The getaway car was—you guessed it—a multicolored Datsun. Bingo! Because the driver's name was already known, officers knew where he lived. They proceeded straight to the house, where they arrested the driver and his four pals.

The suspects were stunned. They couldn't imagine how they had been caught so fast.

He Got a Charge out of It

The General Services Administration (GSA) has its own criminal investigators to handle reports of crimes in federal buildings. One afternoon they received a report that a man was attempting to steal an air conditioner from outside one of the federal buildings in Atlanta. GSA investigators hurried to the scene, but as it turned out they could have taken their time—because they were dealing with a dumb criminal.

This particular genius was using a huge meat cleaver to cut through the various hoses, pipes, and other lines connected to the air conditioner. The cleaver was metal. All metal. No wooden or plastic handles on this baby. It was 100 percent metallic, and it was doing a good job cutting the copper pipe and rubber hoses. Of course, air conditioners run on electricity, and the heavy cleaver did a good job of cutting the electrical lines as well. It also did a good job of conducting the electricity from the electrical lines into the would-be thief, who lit up like a Christmas tree.

When the GSA investigators arrived, they found the dazed and slightly singed suspect lying on the ground, his eyes still rolling around in his head. He offered no resistance, but he made it clear he wanted nothing more to do with that air conditioner.

The heavy cleaver did a good job of cutting the electrical lines as well.

How well do you know the dumb criminal mind?

When released from prison on May 7, 1980, Paul Geidel had spent more consecutive years in a U.S. prison than any other convict in U.S. history. He was seventeen when he walked in. How old was he when he walked out?

a) 60 years old.
b) 77 years old.
c) 85 years old.
d) 93 years old.
e) 101 years old.

The answer is (c). Sentenced to prison for murder on September 5, 1911, Geidel walked out of the Fishkill Correctional Facility in Beacon, New York, a free man after having served sixty-eight years, eight months, and two days. He was eighty-five years old. Do you think his girlfriend waited for him?

On a Losing Streak

Back in those crazy days of the seventies, a college craze known as "streaking" was making the rounds in America. Thousands of students were trying their hand and baring their, well, everything on campuses, at public ceremonies, and in the parks and streets. Sure, it was just a college prank. But the community of Pensacola, Florida, had voted that any kind of public nakedness was offensive enough to merit being against the law, so police officers such as Sgt. Perry Knowles were charged with keeping the streakers off the streets.

Knowles and his partner were on a narcotics stakeout behind an old forties-style downtown hotel when they heard the call. A young man dressed in nothing but red shoes and a cowboy hat had chosen Main Street for an evening run.

Setting out to investigate the general area of the sighting, Knowles noticed something down an alley. A white object had appeared in a hedge about thirty feet down the alley. Knowles hit the spotlight and, with his partner, zeroed in on the Unidentified White Object. The officers didn't need binoculars to identify what it was. Sticking out of the bushes was a large, naked, human, well, posterior. And it was moving slightly, sort of bobbing up and down.

Knowles and his partner quietly walked up to the bobbing rump, noticing the red sneakers down below.

"What are you doing?" they asked.

Without looking up, the college kid tossed off a nonchalant reply, "Oh, I just streaked Main Street, and I can't find my clothes."

"Well, here, I've got a flashlight. Let us help you."

The kid thanked him, took the flashlight, and kept looking down for his shirt and pants and underwear. They found his clothes moments later, and Knowles gave him a ride downtown . . . completely dressed.

Out on a Limb

Birmingham, Alabama, police captain Mike Coppage tells of an unlucky criminal he came across after arriving on the scene at a two-story office building, responding to an attempted break-in. Coppage says "attempted break-in" because the man never got inside the building. In fact, he never actually got *onto* the building.

Captain Coppage walked around to the back of the property, shining his flashlight toward the rooftop. The roof was clear, but a man was standing in a tree right next to the building. Coppage recognized Toby, a well-known small-time thief.

"Toby," Coppage yelled, "get down from there!"

A shaky voice yodeled something back.

"What'd you say, Toby?" Coppage called again.

"I can't get down. I'm stuck," came the reply. He was talking like an amateur ventriloquist.

"You're stuck?"

"Yeah, if I fall from here I'll pull my foot off. Help me."

Coppage took a closer look. Toby had one foot stretched out and wedged tightly behind a drainpipe that ran up the side of the building. His other leg was wobbling on a medium-sized limb about twenty-five feet above the ground. "I don't know how he was managing to stay balanced on that limb," the officer remembers.

Police had to call for a hook-and-ladder truck to get him down. Toby was then arrested and taken to jail for attempted burglary and criminal trespass.

For all his ineptitude as a burglar, though, we think Toby showed great promise as a branch manager.

Mirror Image

Most wild-game poachers work at night in isolated areas. Unless they do something really stupid, odds are they won't get caught. Deputy Sheriff Ronald Saville of Fort Benton, Montana, remembers some elk poachers who would have escaped clean but for a bit of carelessness.

Acting on a tip that someone had been shooting elk in the area, the deputy and a state game warden checked the area. This being the middle of winter, they had no trouble following the blood trail across the snow to where the poachers had gutted the animal. But other than the gory elk remains, there didn't seem to be any useful evidence—until they examined the scene more closely.

There in a snowbank, where the poachers had backed up a truck to load the elk carcass, the officers found an imprint of a license plate. It took only a moment to obtain a registration. The dumb poachers were astonished when met by a law enforcement welcoming committee.

There Will Be an Additional Charge

One time while processing new prisoners at the downtown Birmingham, Alabama, jail, Capt. Arnetta Nunn was frisking a large woman for drugs and weapons when she touched what felt like a gun handle in the woman's girdle.

"What's that?" Nunn asked.

"That's a gun," the woman casually said. "But don't tell anybody I've got it."

"Don't tell anybody? Ma'am, I'm a police officer. I *have* to tell somebody."

Luckily, the woman was just dumb and not crazy.

"Are you right- or left-handed?" Nunn asked.

"I'm right-handed," the woman said.

"All right, then, with your left hand, reach into your girdle. Using your thumb and index finger, very slowly remove the gun from your pants."

In the next moment the officer was holding a fully loaded .38-caliber revolver. To go with the woman's original charges, she was charged with trying to smuggle a weapon into a correctional facility.

Captain Nunn recounts, " 'Don't tell anybody'? Why do I get all the fools?"

38 Do You Know Where Your Children Are?

Deputy Bill Cromie was patrolling the deserted streets of Phoenix, New York, around two in the morning when he noticed a fifteen-year-old boy pushing his bike along the street. Although it was unusual to see someone of that age out on the street at that time of morning, it was something else that drew Cromie's attention. Balanced on the kid's bike was a huge, glass-fronted china cabinet.

Cromie knew the boy. He pulled up beside him and asked the boy what he was doing with the china cabinet. Clearly nervous, the lad stumbled over his words but finally said he was taking the china cabinet home to his mother. Realizing how lame this story sounded, the kid eventually admitted he had stolen it from a house down the street.

"Those people have been away for a long time," he said, "and I didn't think they would miss it. Besides, my mom has always wanted one of these things."

The kid eventually admitted he had stolen it from a house down the street.

Because they were only a block from the boy's house, Cromie followed him home so Cromie could talk to his mother.

The mother answered the door, and Cromie explained he had apprehended her son with a stolen china cabinet. She in turn asked the boy why in the world he would break into that particular house. The kid gave his mother a surprised look. "Don't you remember, Mom? You told me to go get it."

Clearly flustered by his reply, she mumbled and stuttered for a minute, then finally used the same words her son had: "Well, they've been gone a long time, and I always wanted one of those china cabinets. I didn't think they'd miss it."

How Do You Spell "Police"?

Police officer Jerry Wiley was returning to the Birmingham, Alabama, station one evening after having successfully served a warrant on a suspected drug kingpin. Nine other officers were riding with Wiley in the police raid van. All wore solid-black fatigues with the word *Police* stenciled across them in *Sesame Street*-sized letters.

They were driving through a heavy drug-trafficking area when a guy on the corner started waving frantically at the vanload of cops, motioning for them to pull over to the curb.

"What's this guy want?" one of the officers asked.

"I don't know," Wiley responded. "Let's find out."

They pulled over to the curb, and the man walked up to Wiley's window. "Y'all wanna buy some rock?"

"Some rock what?" Wiley asked.

"Rock cocaine, man. I got somethin' really nice here. You gonna love it."

Almost on cue, Wiley and his nine fellow officers

looked at one another incredulously, took another look down at their clearly marked uniforms, then shook their heads in disbelief. Either this guy was illiterate, or he had smoked enough "coke" to suffer brain damage.

Wiley gathered his wits and, struggling to keep a straight face, asked, "Sure, man, whatcha got?"

"I got some twenty-dollar pieces here, man . . . real nice. How many you want?"

Wiley looked at the guys in back, nodded to them, and said, "Well, I guess I'd better take all of 'em."

That was their cue. The doors of the van burst open, and ten armed officers jumped out, shouting, "Police! Freeze! Get on the ground!"

Says Wiley, "You should have seen the look on that guy's face—it was one of sheer terror. I thought he was going to have a heart attack right there."

The intrepid drug salesman was arrested and charged with possession and sale of a controlled substance.

"Were it against the law to be stupid," Wiley says, "we could have charged him with that, too."

They Always Return to the Scene of the Crime

40

It's amazing how many people don't know when they're well off—like the man whom former Baltimore, Maryland, policeman Frank Walmer stopped for erratic driving.

"There was no doubt the guy was drunk," Walmer says. "But he came out of the car just crying his eyes out. He told me he had just been notified that his elderly mother, who had been in Provident Hospital for some time, was about to expire, and he was trying to get there in time to see her one last time."

Walmer asked the man if he had been drinking, and he admitted he had. "I didn't intend to be driving," the man said. "But when the hospital called, I didn't have no other way to get there."

Feeling compassion for the man, Walmer told him to park his car and offered to drive him to the hospital. Blubbering his appreciation, the driver did as he was

321

told. When the two men got to the hospital, the driver thanked Walmer effusively for his help, then dashed inside.

"I was glad to help him, but I have to admit I was a little suspicious," Walmer says. "There was just something about his behavior that didn't ring true."

Wondering if he was becoming too cynical, Walmer drove back to the man's automobile and parked a block away so he could keep an eye on it. Eight minutes later a cab containing the still-intoxicated driver arrived. Out he jumped, keys in hand, and headed for his car.

"I waited until he slid behind the wheel before I pulled in behind him and turned on my lights," Walmer says. "When I walked up to his car, he just shook his head and said, 'I knew this was going to be a bad day.' "

Why I Hate Family Disturbances

Most law enforcement officers hate family disturbance calls. Not only are they frustrating to handle, but
there is also the real possibility that one or both of the
combatants will turn on the interfering officer. Many law
enforcement officers have been injured or killed while
trying to calm down family fights.

Don Parker was a deputy with the Escambia County
Sheriff's Department in Pensacola, Florida, when he
handled a memorable family disturbance call. The address was a second-floor apartment in a two-story building. As Parker climbed the stairs and started down the
outside walkway, he heard yelling and screaming from
the end apartment. The door was standing open about
four inches, and the hoarse tones of an obviously
drunken male were being drowned out by the shrill so-
prano of an enraged female. Parker pounded on the door

and identified himself. There was instant silence but no response, so he pounded again.

"At that point the door flew open and the drunk came charging through like a fullback running for daylight," Parker said. "Unfortunately, I had been a little careless, and instead of standing to one side I was standing directly in front of the door. The drunk charged straight into me, carrying me backward with his rush.

"I had only a brief impression of a very large man wearing blue checkered pajama bottoms and nothing else. He had wild, bloodshot eyes, shaggy hair, and two days' growth of beard. He was at least six inches taller than me and fifty pounds heavier. At the moment of collision, he grabbed me by the arms, pinning them to my side, and we shot across the walkway and crashed into the railing. The force of the assault bent me backward over the rail, and my straw Stetson spun away in the darkness."

The man was so strong that Parker was unable to move. "Put me in jail!" the man shouted. "Just put me in jail!"

"I tried to think of something I could say to quiet him," Parker says. "So I asked him, 'Why do you want to go to jail?' I asked as calmly as I could.

" 'Because I'm drunk!' he shouted, giving me a shake with each word, 'and I belong in jail!'

324

The drunk came charging through like a fullback running for day-light.

"Although I was still completely helpless, I looked him in the eye and said sternly, 'Okay, that's it. You're under arrest.' "

Immediately, a big smile lit up the drunk man's face.

" 'All riiiiight!' he said, releasing me abruptly. He turned and sprinted down the concrete walk, bare feet pounding, ran down the stairs, crossed the parking lot, opened the back door of my cruiser, jumped in, and slammed it behind him!"

By the time Parker got to his car there was nothing more for him to do. He holstered his gun and stood there breathing hard, trying to collect his shattered wits. After a moment the guy in the backseat yelled, "Hey, are we going to jail or what?"

Parker assured him he was indeed going to jail. The man settled back in the backseat and smiled, saying, "It's about damn time."

You Can Run, But . . .

Officer Jay Macintosh was a police sergeant at the time, pulling watch on the streets of Birmingham, Alabama, at four o'clock in the morning, when he pulled up next to a man at a traffic light. Because it was summertime, the guy had all the windows in his car rolled down. There was a light breeze and, when it shifted in Macintosh's direction, it carried the pungent, unmistakable smell of marijuana smoke.

The man then made a right turn on red, which is legal, but he didn't use his turn signal. Macintosh hit his lights, pulled the smoking dope over, and asked the guy to get out of his car and hand over his driver's license. He did.

Macintosh sniffed. The vehicle reeked of pot. "Do you have any objections to my searching your car?" Macintosh asked.

The only answer Macintosh got was the guy taking off running. Macintosh's instincts screamed, *chase him*, but he thought about it for a second and decided to stay put.

"I'm thinking, *I've got this guy's driver's license with his name, address, and picture on it. I know where he lives, and I've got his car, so where's he gonna go?*" Macintosh says. "I felt sorry for the guy, I really did. He seemed like a regular guy who was going through some rough times."

Macintosh was calling for a tow truck when he looked up to see that his runner had come back. "I'm sorry, officer," he told Macintosh. "I just panicked and took off. But I got about a block away and thought, *Wait a minute . . . the cop's got my driver's license and my car, and he's got me.*"

"I was right about him," Macintosh says. "He was a nice guy. He was going through a divorce, and he'd never been arrested in his life."

How 'bout Some Hot Wax with That?

43

It was a routine traffic stop, but Officer Grace Reid of Pensacola, Florida, knew that nothing is ever really routine when it comes to crime. There's always the possibility that the person you're stopping has a less-than-happy history with the law and might decide to do something crazy, so you have to be on your toes.

This particular gentleman seemed nervous from the moment Officer Reid saw him. He stepped from his car and started eating something from his pocket. Either the guy was eating a powdered substance such as cocaine, or he had stashed some powdered-sugar doughnuts for a snack and had decided just to eat the sugar.

Reid grabbed the guy, spun him around, and cuffed him quickly, then spun him back and tried to get whatever it was out of his mouth. If it was what she thought it was and he managed to ingest too much of it, he would probably overdose and she wouldn't have a case.

As she went for his mouth, he went for his coat pocket with his now-cuffed hands. He tossed some more cocaine onto the trunk of Reid's cruiser and spun around, smashing his face onto her trunk in an attempt to scarf down four plastic packets of powder. Reid kept pulling him up, and he kept going back to lick her trunk.

Reid finally got him into the backseat of the cruiser and retrieved enough evidence to arrest and convict him. It was not the first time she had seen a suspect try to eat the evidence, but it was definitely the first time she had had a suspect wash her squad car with his tongue.

Merry-Go-Round

It was a cool April evening in the Florida Panhandle when Officer Tony Jordan spotted a couple in a pickup veering all over the road. The gentleman at the wheel would slowly fade over into the oncoming lane and then suddenly jerk back into his lane.

Officer Jordan caught up with them and signaled for them to pull over. With some difficulty, they pulled into the parking lot of a shopping center. As Jordan walked toward the vehicle, Jordan could hear the couple arguing.

After the man stepped from the car, Jordan asked the driver's wife, who also seemed intoxicated and a bit peeved, to stay put and not to start or move the vehicle. Jordan administered the field sobriety test to the man, who failed miserably. The man pleaded with the officer not to arrest him and insisted that his wife had had less to drink and was therefore capable of driving them both home.

Sure enough, as he spoke the words, the guy's wife

fired up that old truck and started to pull away, slowly. The officer cuffed the man and told him not to move, then jumped into his squad car to follow her. With lights flashing and siren sounding, he pursued the woman who was just a few car lengths ahead of him and barely moving.

"Stop the truck, ma'am, and turn off the key!" Jordan bellowed over his loudspeaker. But the woman just kept fleeing at ten miles per hour.

"Ma'am, please stop the truck!" Jordan yelled repeatedly, in between calls for backup. "Stop the truck and turn off the key!"

By this time Jordan was getting nauseous. After about ten minutes of this grueling, extremely low-speed chase in circles, the woman veered toward the mall and almost struck a building. Three other cruisers closed in and surrounded the fleeing motorist. When they opened the door to the pickup, the woman fell out and had to be supported. The loops mixed with the alcohol had gotten to her, too.

When it was all over, Officer Jordan and both his suspects took a slow, straight drive to the jail.

A Fool and His Tools Are Soon Parted

Lt. Jay Macintosh of Birmingham, Alabama, was working at the East Precinct at the time. He had just received a call from one of the officers at the North Precinct asking if Macintosh was familiar with a guy named Troy, a local burglar. Macintosh said yes, he had arrested Troy in the past. Well, this time it seems there had just been a break-in at a Sears store, and Troy's wallet had been found at the scene.

"I knew where Troy lived," Macintosh says, "so I went over to his house to see if he was around. I'd just pulled up and turned off my lights when here comes Troy down the street in his car. When he gets closer, he sees me sitting there and slows down. Then he just stops his car.

"I get out of my squad car, walk up to his window, and say, 'Troy, let me see your driver's license, please.' "

Troy began feeling around in his back pockets and then

started patting his shirt pockets and looking around on the seat. "I can't find my wallet, officer," he said.

"I didn't think you would," Macintosh said.

"You didn't?"

"Nope. I didn't."

Macintosh began to shine his light into the backseat of Troy's car. It was loaded with new power tools.

"Hey, Troy, let me ask you something, man. You got a sander I could borrow?"

Old Troy just hung his head. He stepped out of the car and put his wrists together.

"By the way," Macintosh told him, "we've got your wallet down at the station."

The Kickstand Caper

Dennis Larsen was a motorcycle cop in Las Vegas in the seventies when he ran into a unique law enforcement situation.

Larsen was making a routine traffic stop in Vegas at about ten o'clock one night. He pulled over a speeding pickup and parked his motorcycle on the side of the road with the kickstand down on the semi-soft shoulder. Officer Larsen was at the driver's-side window of the pickup asking for the man's driver's license and registration when he heard the horrible, unmistakable sound of a heavy, well-equipped police motorcycle crashing to the pavement. His kickstand had broken.

Now, police motorcycles are not your little, lightweight dirt bikes. They are big, heavy machines. Larsen asked the speeding motorist to help him get his bike up off the shoulder of the road. Then Larsen hopped on and began to make a beeline for the police garage.

On the way to the garage, unfortunately, he spotted a

little street bike zipping in and out of lanes, cutting people off, and generally being extremely reckless. There was no way Larsen could stop anyone without an operational kickstand on his bike, but the guy driving the street bike was being a real jerk.

Finally, Larsen flipped on his lights and siren and gave chase. The biker pulled over in the next block. Larsen pulled over behind him. Larsen, still sitting on his bike, raised one hand and motioned for the man to come over to his bike. "I want you to straddle the front tire of my bike and grab my handlebars with both hands," Larsen said.

The man looked puzzled but did as he was told. Then Larsen finally was able to let go of his bike and step off. He asked for the man's license, and the gentleman explained it was in his wallet in his back pocket. Larsen retrieved the wallet and the license, while the man kept a firm grip on the handlebars. Larsen then began writing the ticket.

After the paperwork was done, he placed his ticket book on his bike's front bumper and again took the handlebars.

"Now, please sign the ticket, sir," Larsen said.

The man let go of the handlebars and signed his ticket.

"Now, please put your hands back on the handlebars, sir."

The man did exactly as he was told and grabbed the bike again. Larsen tore off the man's copy of the ticket and stuffed it in the guy's shirt pocket. He then took the handlebars back from the biker and hopped onto his bike.

"You know," the man said, "I've been stopped before, but nobody has ever made me stand like that and grab the handlebars. Is that some new thing the cops do now?"

"No, sir. My kickstand broke about ten minutes ago, and I was on my way to the police garage to get it fixed."

The man scratched his head again. "So, what would you have done if I hadn't stopped?"

"All I would have been able to do was radio it in and follow you until I ran out of gas."

"What would you have done if I had dropped your bike and made a run for it?"

"Well, my bike weighs too much for me to pick it up and chase you, so I couldn't have followed you."

DUMB CRIMINAL QUIZ NO. 417

How well do you know the dumb criminal mind?

With such illicit drugs as cocaine, crystal "meth," and even heroin so prevalent in our society, a recent study was done in Los Angeles to determine what percentage, if any, of the paper money in circulation might be tainted with traces of these drugs. (Bills collect residue when they are rolled up and used as straws to snort the drugs.) What percentage did the study reveal?

a) 3 percent
b) 75 percent
c) 51 percent
d) 18 percent
e) 0 percent

The answer is (b). A whopping 75 percent of all paper money tested in Los Angeles contained trace amounts of these drugs!

It's Later than You Think

Detective Jerry Wiley of Birmingham, Alabama, offers this story of stupidity concerning a man who entered a convenience store and told the young female cashier to back away from the register.

"Don't hit that button under there, either," he told her.

"How do you know what that button is?" she asked.

"Honey, I've been robbin' these here little stores since before you were born, that's how I know. I robbed my first one at the tender age of eleven."

The man took the money from the drawer, casually counted it, and stuffed it into his pocket. He then winked at the young girl as he opened the door to leave and said, "You'd have to get up pretty early in the morning to catch old Bo Ramsey!"

When the police arrived, the cashier described the man and repeated what he had said. They ran his name through the computer and got a copy of his driver's license, with picture I.D., which they showed the clerk.

"Yep, that's him. That's the pro."

48 Dumber Indemnity

Having just received an eviction notice from his landlady for nonpayment of rent, Henry came up with a brilliant idea that would allow him to, one, get revenge on his landlady and, two, grab some real cash! All he needed was a renter's insurance policy and a couple of cans of gas.

Henry bought an insurance policy with a benefit of ten thousand dollars. He then informed all his Pensacola, Florida, neighbors that he had to take a short trip out of town and would be back in a couple of days. No one would ever suspect!

He returned after dark, parked his car around the block, took two five-gallon gasoline cans from his trunk, and made his way stealthily through a wooded lot behind the house. Creeping to an open window, he poured in the ten gallons of gasoline. All he had to do now was let the gasoline soak in a bit, throw a match through the window, and saunter back to his car.

All he had to do now was let the gasoline soak in a bit.

Unfortunately, gasoline does more than soak in; it fills any space with explosive fumes very quickly. Henry threw the match through the window and gave new meaning to the term "shotgun shack."

Brushing pieces of the house off himself, Henry limped to his car. Meanwhile, a quick-thinking neighbor who saw him had called 911. A patrolman, hearing the dispatcher's description of the car, quickly spotted Henry and pulled him over.

When the patrolman asked Henry to step out of his car, he was overpowered by the smell of pine. "Someone just set my house on fire, and I'm trying to catch him!" Henry told the officer. The officer, shining his flashlight into Henry's car, saw a can of pine air freshener on the seat.

"I see," the officer said. "What kind of car was he driving?"

As Henry continued his story, unfortunately, his pine cologne began to fade, giving way to the distinctive odor of gasoline.

On what must have been a long ride to the station, he asked the patrolman, "Do you think they'll still pay on my insurance policy?"

Dumber than That Even

Detective Buddy Tidwell, now of Nashville, Tennessee, started out his career on the small police force of a quiet rural community.

One evening Buddy got a call from a neighbor describing one of the most unusual thefts in county history. It seems that Mr. McDonald had dropped off a truckload of hay about eighty miles away in the next county. Coming back, his truck had started to overheat, so McDonald had pulled over near a stream to give the forty-year-old Ford a cool drink from the creek. That's when three joyriding punks pulled up and decided to give Ol' McDonald a rough time.

"Hey, ol' man, nice ride," they hooted. "You must be one of them rich farmers with a million bucks stuffed in his mattress in an old sock, right?"

McDonald just shook his head and muttered under his breath, but he wasn't really in a position to fight off the three of them. So the punks took the old man's wallet and ran.

Going through the wallet, the punks discovered not only McDonald's hay money, but also the receipts for a VCR and a big-screen TV he had just purchased. The thugs decided to call the phone number they had also found in the wallet. McDonald answered. The punks said they knew where he lived and that they wanted his new TV and VCR. If McDonald didn't put all the new merchandise into a box on the lawn before nine that night, they said, they would come in and get him and his wife. The old farmer finally called the police. Buddy Tidwell took the call.

"The old guy was pretty scared, so we told him to get his family out of there and down to the station immediately," Tidwell says. "Then we rolled."

When the officers got to the house, they hid their cars. Buddy found the empty boxes for the TV and VCR still sitting in the garage. His partner helped him fill up the boxes with the first thing they could find in the garage—paving stones, lots of 'em. They quickly duct-taped the boxes up and slid them onto the lawn in front of the house. Then they took up positions in the bushes and waited.

Right on schedule, the punks pulled up, driving slowly with their headlights turned off. The three youths got out of the car, then tried to lift the biggest box of rocks.

"It probably weighed two hundred fifty pounds," Tidwell says, "but these boys managed to get it up and started to run, well, walk real fast with it."

The officers let the punks get pretty far along before they called out and identified themselves. They called for the fleeing thieves to stop, but the fools wouldn't. Instead, they changed direction and tried to jog into the woods with their heavy loot.

"We just kind of jogged behind them," Tidwell says. "We never got too close because we wanted them to carry that box as far as they could."

The criminals finally just wore out and collapsed, giving themselves up to Buddy and his partner. The officers couldn't wait to show them just what they had risked their lives to drag through the woods.

"At that point," remembers Buddy, "they definitely felt dumber than a box of rocks."

 **50**

Should Have Stayed in Seventh Grade

A man presented himself to Sgt. Thomas Pennington at Las Vegas, Nevada, police headquarters to inquire as to why a narcotics detective had been looking for him. There was a one-million-dollar, drug-trafficking charge outstanding on the man in California, but he assumed he couldn't be arrested for it in another state. The desk sergeant explained the law to him as he snapped on the cuffs.

The One-Armed Orangutan

51

The ownership of exotic pets often seems to lead to frantic calls of one sort or another to police. One began as a routine burglary call. When Officer Ronnie Allen of Oklahoma City, Oklahoma, arrived at the apartment, he was greeted by an elderly gentleman. Senior citizens are all too often easy prey for burglars and other criminals, so Allen was feeling bad for the guy while he began the routine process of listing the stolen items. Then the old gent made a startling statement.

"But what I'm really worried about is my one-armed orangutan. He can get downright nasty when he's not fed."

"Your what, sir?"

"My one-armed orangutan. He's only about four-foot-six, but apes are unusually strong for their size, especially a one-armed ape. His left arm is as strong as three men's arms."

"You had a one-armed orangutan here?"

"Till he got stolen or ran off. He was here when I left. One of these burgers was for him. He'll be angry that he didn't get his burger."

At this point, Allen didn't know if the old guy was confused, pulling his leg, or the genuine owner of a missing one-armed orangutan. It's not something you want to call in without being really sure of what you're saying. But the old guy's story was confirmed when Allen heard a disturbance call from an apartment nearby. It seems a group of larcenous individuals were sitting around taking inventory of the items they had just stolen from the old man's apartment. The burglars were also inhaling toxic paint fumes to "cop a cheap buzz."

Unfortunately for them, the cracked crooks had forced a certain one-armed orangutan, who just happened to be hanging out with them, to sniff the paint, too. The drugged-out ape had gone berserk and was wreaking havoc in the apartment. The police had to get the old man to talk the orangutan out so that the burglars could give themselves up to police without being torn apart.

The Long Windshield of the Law

52

Veteran officer Johnny Cooley of Birmingham, Alabama, had been patrolling the same stretch of interstate highway for twenty-four years. He had seen it all on this one small portion of superslab. As with a lot of the officers we've interviewed, though, no stories sprang immediately to his mind. So we took a little ride with him.

As he drove us down the otherwise unremarkable stretch of highway, memories and stories started flooding back with each mile marker we passed. When we passed the one marked "38," he suddenly started to laugh . . . and we mean belly laughs, the kind that bring tears to your eyes. This is the story he told of the bust at mile marker 38.

The officer was actually off duty and was just headed home in the right-hand lane of a four-lane highway. His radar gun was off, he was off the clock, and as far as he was concerned he was just another guy driving home from work. He was, however, the only guy on the highway driving a police cruiser home.

Out of the corner of his eye, he noticed a car swerving erratically and then speeding up in the left lane. The officer watched as the car kept accelerating, veering in and out of lanes, narrowly missing several cars. The four men in the car, obviously, had either done something wrong or they were intoxicated . . . or both. So the officer called in the incident on his radio and fell in behind the speeding car with his lights lit and the siren screaming.

The guys in the car sped up. They shot in between cars, veered out onto the shoulder, and darted back up onto the road, trying to lose the trailing cop. Eventually, the officer noticed that the two men in the backseat were tossing something out the windows. An object hit the police cruiser's windshield as other items flew past the squad car. Then, suddenly, the fleeing car pulled over, right by mile marker 38.

The officer cautiously approached the car and asked the occupants to step out. The four men complied willingly, coyly acting as though they had no idea why the officer had stopped them.

"What was that stuff you guys were throwing out the window?"

The officer knew it had to be drugs, but there were no drugs in the car, and none of the men had drugs on his person.

An object hit the police cruiser's windshield as other items flew past the squad car.

"Aw, that was just a cigarette pack," one lousy liar said while grinning really big. "I'm sorry. I guess you got me for littering." The other passengers laughed.

As his backup arrived, the officer took the four men's licenses back to his squad car to run a check for prior arrests or any outstanding warrants. That's when he noticed the object lodged on the windshield wiper of his squad car. Reaching over, he plucked off an overstuffed bag of marijuana.

The dopers had scored a direct hit, but it was the officer who hit the jackpot. He had collared four of the biggest dealers in the city. No one was laughing now—except for the officer, of course.

Calling All Cops

Beepers can be a disadvantage for dumb crooks in more ways than one. Such was the experience of an undercover narcotics officer in Florida nurturing a relationship with a known drug dealer who was a first-class slimeball and a major source of crack cocaine.

Making a narcotics buy without entrapment and with as much admissible evidence as possible is the goal of every undercover narcotics investigation. This particular officer had socialized; that is, he had seen and been seen in all the right places by his target. Gradually, over a two-month period, he had developed a relationship with the dealer. Finally, the officer had made his first buy, and he and the dealer had exchanged pager numbers so they could arrange future transactions.

The stage was set for a second buy. If this operation was done properly, the cops would then have cash, drugs, audio recordings, still photographs, and video on this guy—hopefully enough to convict him of drug trafficking and put him away.

But then the suspect made an interesting mistake. He called the undercover officer's pager to alert his "customer" that the stuff was in and the deal was going down, but he got the last number of the officer's beeper number wrong. The number he accidentally dialed just happened to be the pager number for the police department's S.W.A.T. team. Eighteen heavily armed, highly trained, sharpshooting officers answer that number.

Luckily, our undercover officer was also a member of the S.W.A.T. team, so he got the beep. And like all of the other seventeen S.W.A.T. team members, he answered the page by calling the number that appeared on his pager. Only when he recognized the answering voice as his dealer did the officer figure out what was going on. He quickly switched into his undercover persona.

"Hey, man, is it going down?"

By now the dealer was totally confused and totally paranoid, because by now he had already talked to about five officers who were answering the S.W.A.T. team page by calling the dealer's home number from the page and identifying themselves. Every cop in town seemed to be calling his number, and he had no idea why.

"Who is this?" he demanded of the undercover officer.

"It's me, Jimmy T.," the narcotics officer said, giving his drug-buying pseudonym.

"Man, I beeped you about ten minutes ago, and then the cops started calling. I ain't kidding, man. Five cops have called here in the last five minutes!"

Now the officer was scrambling to fix any possible damage. Luckily, he had himself a bona fide dumb criminal. "Wait, what number did you call?" he asked.

The dealer told him, and he laughed. "You got the last number wrong. My pager number ends in seven, not eight. You must've called the cops!"

"I must have."

"Did you say anything?" the officer said, fearing his cover had been blown and fishing for information.

"No! I just told them that it must've been a wrong number."

"Whoa, dude. Close call. So, do you have the stuff?"

The dealer and the undercover officer met within the hour, and as they did their business they both laughed about the erroneous beep. Their laughter was captured on audio and videotape along with the deal that convicted the dealer.

The Bare Facts

Working radar on a blistering summer's day is not the job assignment of choice for most law enforcement officers. It was just such a day that Officer Bill Cromie was running radar in a small town in upstate New York.

"I was sitting right by the side of the road with my air conditioning running, letting the sight of my marked car slow the speeding drivers and actually blinking my headlights at some of the faster ones," Cromie says.

So far he had been able to avoid having to actually write a single ticket. But he could see off in the distance a car approaching at a high rate of speed. Cromie blinked his headlights, but the vehicle didn't slow.

Cromie set off in pursuit. By the time he caught up to the speeder, she was still doing over fifty miles per hour. When she saw his blue lights, she pulled over. Cromie got out of his car, ticket book in hand, and then did a double take.

"Looking through the rear window I could see she was alone in the car, but she seemed to be shrinking. With each step that I took, she slid that much lower in the front seat. I was about to ask for her driver's license, but I only got as far as, 'May I see your—' because I suddenly realized I could see her—*all* of her. The woman was stark naked."

At that point it was hard to say who was more embarrassed and, blushing furiously, Cromie turned his back on the cringing woman. "I suppose I was taking a risk, but I was fairly sure she wasn't carrying any concealed weapons. Of course, I asked her how it was that she came to be driving her car, naked, at a high rate of speed."

The woman told him that she had been driving beside a river, and it had looked so cool and inviting that she just had to take a quick swim. Picking what she thought was a deserted section, she had peeled off her sweaty clothing and dived in. The water had been wonderful, but as she floated with the current she had seen two fishermen emerge from bushes and sit on the bank only a few feet from where she had left her clothes. Intent on catching fish, they hadn't seen her or her clothes, but they obviously had posed a major problem for the swimmer.

From the looks of things, they had settled in for the day.

Luckily, the woman's keys were still in the car, so she had swum around a bend in the river and waded ashore, creeping past the unsuspecting fishermen. She had been able to get to her car undetected and was headed for home when Cromie stopped her.

Convinced she had to be telling the truth, he said he would let her go without writing her a ticket. The woman expressed her gratitude, but wanted to know if Cromie had a coat she could borrow. He didn't. Unhappy with his answer, she insisted that he help her.

"I told her the only thing I could give her was my uniform, but that would have been pretty hard to explain if she got stopped again. She finally drove off, still hunkered down in the seat. But at least she was doing the speed limit."

Fooled You

Police captain Arnetta Nunn of Birmingham, Alabama, is a real charmer, so much so that one dumb criminal actually sought her out.

Nunn was working in plain clothes and driving an unmarked car at the time. She had just walked out of city hall and crossed the street to her car when a man approached her from behind.

"You want to buy some rings?" he asked Nunn. "I stole these in Tennessee."

"You stole them?" Nunn asked.

"Yeah, up in Tennessee, and I really need some money right now, so I'm sellin' 'em real cheap. This stuff is top of the line."

Well, Nunn took a look at some of the rings and found them to be cheapo stuff with high-dollar tags.

"I picked up one ring and kind of held it up to my eye," Nunn remembers, "and he says, 'Don't let the man see you!' He was nervous and kept looking around, and then he looked down into the front seat of the car and saw the police radio on the floorboard."

At this point the man asked Nunn if she was with the police. She answered in the affirmative.

"You ain't got nothin' on me," he said self-assuredly. "This stuff ain't stolen, and I can prove it. So, ha! You can't touch me. You're a fool, lady."

That made Nunn mad, especially the "fool" part. Here's some two-bit con man out here on the streets scamming people's hard-earned money from them and telling Nunn there was nothing she could do about it. She was determined to prove him wrong.

"You want to walk over to city hall with me and find out who the real fool is?" Nunn asked him.

"Sure, I'll go over there with you. I told you, you can't touch me."

Nunn and her newfound acquaintance walked across the street. Every step of the way, Nunn was thinking, *What can I nail this guy on? If he can prove those rings are really his, then there goes that charge.* They walked into city hall, where Nunn told him to just have a seat and she'd be right back to book him.

Just then a veteran of twenty years walked up and asked Nunn what she had out in the hall. She explained the situation to him, and he casually said, "There's a city ordinance that prohibits the sale of merchandise on the street within a six-block radius of the downtown loop without a license. Does he have one?"

Holding back a chuckle, Nunn walked back out into the hallway and said to the man, "Do you have a license to sell that junk in the loop area?"

Stunned silence.

"I didn't think so. Follow me, please."

"Follow you where?" he asked with a puzzled look.

"Back to the booking room. You're under arrest for failure to procure a city license to sell in the loop area. C'mon, fool."

56 What's in a Name?

Retired FBI agent Fred McFaul remembers when he was a young and newly assigned agent in Florida. A veteran agent had been working a bomb threat extortion case and asked Fred to come along while he interviewed the suspect. The case involved an unknown person who had been demanding money from a local business and threatening to blow up the business if the demands were not met. The suspect was a man named Robert Moore.

"We drove to the suspect's house, located in a small town in northwest Florida," McFaul says. "The guy was quite willing to talk with us."

The two agents had a long and rambling conversation with Robert Moore, but made no real headway. He continued to deny that he had anything to do with the bomb threats. Also, they were having a bit of a communication problem.

"I was from the North," McFaul says, "and I had a little trouble understanding the suspect's southern accent.

Every so often, I would have to ask him to repeat something."

Our suspect was in the process of telling the two agents how innocent he was, when he again said something that McFaul did not catch. "It sounded like he said, 'All these people, they be saying that Bomb Moore been making them threats, but it ain't true.' Now, I knew his name was Robert, and I thought he must have said *Bob,* but it really did sound like *Bomb.* I asked him to repeat the name he had called himself, and his eyes suddenly got real big."

The suspect hemmed and hawed for a few minutes. Finally, he admitted that the word was indeed *Bomb,* but that it was only a nickname.

"I asked him how he came to have such an explosive nickname," McFaul says, "and by then he was starting to sweat. A little more prodding, and he admitted he had been given the name because as a young man he liked to 'blow things up.' "

After that, it didn't take the agents long to obtain a full and complete confession.

57 Fail Safe

It was after midnight in Illinois when two thieves finally made it to the second floor of an old office building. It had taken them more than an hour to cut a hole in the roof big enough for the two very large men to squeeze through.

It was a hot summer night, and they were already sweating profusely by the time they found the three-hundred-pound safe in the manager's office. Within minutes, one was cutting around the door frame with an acetylene torch while the other was attempting to knock the tumbler off the safe with a sledgehammer. After forty-five minutes they were exhausted. They couldn't get it open.

"I've got an idea," one of them said. "Let's take it over to the window and drop it into the alley. With all the damage we've done to it, it should bust wide open when it hits!"

After pouring some water from the office cooler on the

"With all the damage we've done to it, it should bust wide open when it hits!"

safe to cool it down, they dragged, pushed, and lifted the steaming safe up to an open window and shoved it out.

The safe landed below with a tremendous crash and clanging sound as it hit the garbage cans. The men quickly ducked down as if they were two little kids who had just beaned somebody with a water balloon. After a moment or two they peeked out. Apparently, nobody had heard.

The two persistent thieves huffed downstairs and broke out through a back door. They hurried down the alley, jumped into their pickup, and pulled up next to the safe. With their adrenaline still pumping hard, they managed to hoist the hot safe into the back of the truck. Then they drove it out of town about twenty miles until they came to a railroad crossing.

"It's 2:20 now," one of them said to the other. "In about ten minutes the CSX [train] out of Decatur is gonna come roaring by here at about sixty miles an hour. So we put the safe on the tracks, the train hits it, and, *pow*, it busts wide open. The engineer will never know he hit anything."

"You're a genius, man," his friend acknowledged.

So with some more huffing and puffing the two brainiacs managed to wrestle the safe out of the truck and onto the railroad tracks. And not a moment too soon.

"Here she comes!" the first man announced. Both of

them hurried off the tracks and ran to duck behind the truck.

It happened just like the crook had predicted. The train's engineer never knew he'd hit anything. He didn't slow down a notch. The speeding train struck the safe at sixty miles per hour just as planned. But instead of bursting open and being tossed aside, the safe caught on the front of the train and was carried off down the tracks into the night. The two men stared in silent disbelief at the fading caboose light. They looked at each other. Neither one spoke. They got into the truck and went home.

But the story was not yet over. Unbeknownst to the two men, a woman had heard the two thieves as they were loading the safe into the back of the truck in the alley. She had taken down their license number and phoned the police, who showed up the following day to arrest them. The safe was found at a switching yard in the next town.

# I Was Only Trying to Help . . . Myself

Officer Ernest Burt was once called to a break-in at a jewelry store in Birmingham, Alabama, during, appropriately, a terrible ice storm. Because few people were able to get around that night, the thieves figured the police wouldn't be able to, either. Wrong.

When Burt et al arrived at the scene, they saw that the front window had been knocked out of the store. Several people could be seen walking around inside the place. Burt and his fellow officers entered the store through the broken window and promptly arrested the six people inside.

"We had gone back into the store to try and find something with which to block up the window, when one of the officers turned to me and said, 'There's still somebody in here,' " Burt says. "I've been a police officer long enough to know that when another cop gets that feeling in his stomach, you pay attention to it. So we looked around some more and, sure enough, we found two more intruders. Then we found another one hiding in the back. That brought the grand total to nine. You've got to listen to those gut feelings."

All nine men arrested were carrying jewelry and watches in their pockets, and yet they still denied being in there to rob the place. Every one of them said he had just gone in to stop the others from taking anything and that he was only trying to help. Right.

"We heard them arguing among themselves later and discovered that the lookout man had gotten cold and gone inside to warm up," Burt says. Then he laughs, "We put them all on ice."

59 I Dare You

Ah, spring, when young people's minds turn to thoughts of Spring Fest. The first warm days bring out thousands of college students eager to celebrate the end of winter. Oswego County (New York) Deputy Sheriff Bill Cromie remembers one particular Spring Fest that had all the required ingredients: a beautiful day, ten thousand thirsty college students, and a few hundred kegs of beer.

Although Cromie was off duty that day, he and the rest of the department were called in to back up the shift deputies trying to deal with a near riot caused by too many young people and too much alcohol at one site. By the time Cromie arrived, the celebration had been halted and the drunken celebrants told to disperse.

A bus company had been hired to transport the kids, and the deputies were allowing the buses to enter the party area one at a time to pick up their loads of passengers. One at a time the buses would travel down the single road, fill up with students, then return along the same road while deputies held up the traffic to allow them to pass.

"The kids were still yelling and shouting and screaming and laughing," Cromie says, "and most of the poor bus drivers looked about done in. But then another bus approached, and the bus driver actually looked happy. I was surprised, because this bus seemed to have the wildest bunch of all. They were hanging out of every window, screaming their heads off, and pounding on the sides of the vehicle. Still, I got a good look at the driver, and there he was with a big smile on his face. I remember thinking that at least here was one guy who was enjoying himself. I also noticed the number on the bus as it passed us. It was 105."

Cromie and his buddies continued to direct traffic, and a short while later a man approached him on foot. "I saw he was wearing a shirt and tie, which was unusual, and that he didn't look too happy. He said that he was a bus driver, but his bus was missing, and he thought some of the college kids had stolen it. I asked him what the number was. It was 105."

It took Deputy Cromie only a moment to radio ahead, and within five minutes the hijacked bus had been stopped. Because Cromie was the only one who had gotten a good look at the driver, he had to identify him.

"Of course, it was one of the students, and he was

drunk as a skunk. He told me the other kids had offered him five bucks each to take the bus, and they had dared him as well."

The temptation had been irresistible, and when a hat full of money was dropped into his lap, the student had succumbed. Now filled with remorse, he apologized for taking the bus and offered to give all the money to the bus driver if he wouldn't press charges. Cromie said it was too late for that and, besides, there was the small matter of the D.U.I. charge.

As the kid was being handcuffed, he tried to explain his actions one more time. "But you don't understand," he wailed. "They dared me to do it!"

Dogged Determination

Sgt. Doug Baldwin of Pensacola's (Florida) finest was working narcotics one hot summer day when he observed a man in a blue Camaro making a drug buy. While other officers closed in on the dealer, Baldwin chased the customer. The customer, unable to lose the officer in his Camaro, jumped from his car and scampered away on foot with Baldwin in pursuit.

Baldwin watched as the man scaled a tall chain-link fence and crept under a car parked within the fenced compound. He kept on watching as the man, shirtless in the heat, began to squirm and fidget under the car. *Ants,* Baldwin said to himself. *Might as well let him lie there a minute.*

Baldwin then heard the sound he had been waiting for—the low, menacing growl of two Dobermans. The fugitive hadn't noticed—even though he used it for a foothold—the large red sign on the fence: Guard Dogs on Duty.

An Ice Guy

Officer Ernest Burt was executing a search warrant for an armed robber and going through the Birmingham, Alabama, house for the third time when he happened to look up and notice that a square of the false ceiling had been moved. Aha!

Right below the ceiling square was a large chest-style freezer, so Burt stepped up onto it to have a look up past the ceiling. Then he thought, *Wait a minute*. He stepped down off the freezer and opened the lid. Gotcha! The man he was looking for was sitting there with his arms wrapped around his legs, rocking back and forth. His skin had turned ashen, and his lips were blue.

"He'd been in there a good twenty minutes," Burt remembers. "If he'd sat in there for another twenty minutes he might have died. He was really very lucky."

Burt took Mr. Freeze out of the freezer and put him in the cooler.

His skin had turned ashen, and his lips were blue.

62 **Safety First**

As a police officer in Baltimore, Maryland, during the sixties, Frank Walmer ran into his share of dumb criminals, including one who had a penchant for robbing mom-and-pop grocery stores. His weapon of choice was a sawed-off shotgun.

"It looked like an oversized handgun, but it was an old-fashioned twelve-gauge with a hammer," Walmer remembers. "There was nothing left of the stock except the pistol grip, and the barrel was no more than six inches long. It didn't even have a trigger guard. This guy hadn't shot anyone yet, but he was getting bolder with each robbery. We figured it was just a matter of time before someone got hurt."

It happened at the very next robbery. Picking out a small grocery store on the west side of town, he came charging through the door, like Jesse James, waving his sawed-off shotgun and making everyone lie on the floor. He scooped up the few dollars in the register, then

He came charging through the door, like Jesse James, waving his
sawed-off shotgun.

backed out the door, sweeping the shotgun back and forth and glaring menacingly at the terrified elderly owner and his equally frightened wife. Pausing in the door for dramatic effect, he aimed the shotgun at the trembling man and said, "Old man, I'm leaving now. And you better not call the cops for ten minutes, or I'll come back and kill you."

Wide-eyed with terror, the man nodded.

"You understand what I'm talking about?" the robber shouted.

"Yes," the owner managed to croak.

"Yes, what?" the bad guy said, cocking the hammer.

"Yes, sir," the man squeaked.

The robber smiled. "That's better. Now don't move, and no one will get hurt." With that, he jammed the shotgun into his belt, catching the trigger on his pants and causing the weapon to discharge.

"Me and one of the sergeants got there at the same time," Walmer says. "We found the guy lying on the ground, moaning. The sergeant examined the wound, and the guy asked him if he was going to die. The sergeant shook his head and said, 'No, you're not going to die. But when you get out of prison, you might want to try for a job with the Vienna Boys Choir.'"

No Brain, No Gain

Police on a stakeout in North Carolina observed a man breaking into a transmission shop by smashing in and climbing through a back window. The police rushed in to arrest him, only to discover that he had broken into a restroom that provided no entry into the building. In a rare instance of the dumb criminal getting a break, the man could not be charged with breaking and entering—because the restroom door hadn't been locked. He was charged with destruction of property.

Three Days of the Convict

Officer Kevin Studyvin of the Birmingham (Alabama) Task Force tells of the time he and his partner were working on a Saturday afternoon, wearing plain clothes and operating out of an unmarked car. As they pulled up to a red light, Studyvin noticed a familiar-looking man on the other side of the intersection. The man across the way made eye contact and began to wave as if he wanted them to pull over. So they did.

"I know you guys are cops, and Saturday must be your day off," he said, "so I figure y'all must be over here in the neighborhood wanting to have a little fun. I've got what you need right here. Y'all want somethin'?"

"Let's do it," Studyvin said, glancing at his partner.

So they did a deal right there.

"We handed him the money, he handed us the dope, and we arrested him," Studyvin says. "No wonder he looked so familiar. We had just busted him for selling us cocaine . . . on Wednesday!"

The Jewel Fool

It was late in the afternoon when a seventy-five-year-old woman entered the Las Vegas, Nevada, police station accompanied by her thirty-five-year-old boyfriend. She was dressed nicely and spoke in a quiet tone as she spoke to an officer about a robbery that had just occurred. Her diamond jewelry was missing.

"If you'll step over to this counter, I'll be glad to take your report," said Carolyn Green, the clerk at the front desk. "Your friend will have to sit over there, though, because only one person at a time is allowed in this area."

The woman's young male companion complied and took a seat in one of the chairs against the waiting-area wall.

"You were robbed, ma'am?" Green asked.

"Yes, I was," she replied. "At my house . . . about ten thousand dollars' worth of diamonds was taken from my house."

After taking down the rest of the necessary information

to start the paperwork, Green asked the woman, "Do you have any idea who it was that robbed you?"

"Yes, I do," came the response.

"Do you know the person's name?"

"Yes, I know his name."

"Would you know him if you saw him again?"

Again, the answer was in the affirmative.

"Do you know where the person is and where we might be able to find him right now?"

The elderly woman looked over her shoulder. "He's sitting right over there against the wall," she said, pointing to her male companion. Green stood up and looked over at the man who had just brought the woman to the station.

"*He's* the man who robbed you?" Green asked in shocked disbelief.

"Yep. My jewels were missing, and I told him I was going to go down to the police station to report it. I asked him to come along, and he said yes, he'd even give me a ride down here. So he did, and here we are."

Green shook her head and called over to the young man. "Sir, will you step over here, please?" The man stood and walked over to the counter.

"Yes?" he said nonchalantly.

"Did you steal this woman's jewelry?"

"I did," he said.

"One moment please, sir," the clerk said. She turned to summon an officer. "This man just admitted that he robbed this woman of ten thousand dollars' worth of jewelry, and now she's signing a complaint against him."

The summoned officer shook *his* head. "Didn't you just come in here with her?"

"Yes," the young man answered blankly.

"She says you're responsible for her missing jewelry."

"She's right," he admitted. "I did it."

"Well, then, you're under arrest for robbery," the still-stunned officer told him.

"Okay," the man sighed, placing his hands over his head and surrendering without incident. He was later sent to prison.

The police probably could have recovered plenty of rocks had they been able to open the man's head.

66 Brown-Bagging It

At about noon on a sultry North Carolina summer day, homicide investigator Darryl Price tells us, hundreds of motorists observed a man walking along a busy six-lane highway wearing a brown paper bag over his head, creating a hazard as he stumbled in front of traffic. Motorists used their car phones to alert police.

The man eventually entered a bank and began to shout. Several tense seconds went by. Someone finally asked, "I'm sorry, what did you say?" With no mouth-hole, the bag-it bandit could not be understood.

Apparently very nervous, the man constantly turned his head, trying to watch everyone in the room. However, his bag did not turn with his head, so most of his time was spent realigning his eyeholes and, of course, repeating himself.

Money in hand, the robber stumbled blindly into six lanes of lunchtime traffic, narrowly avoiding being run down. He was quickly bagged by police.

He stumbled in front of traffic. Motorists used their car phones to
alert police.

Don't I Know You from Somewhere?

Lt. Kirk Williams of the Randall County Sheriff's Department in Canyon, Texas, ran into a dumb criminal who apparently thought everyone's memory was as bad as his. This fellow walked into a store one morning and paid for his purchase with a check. The clerk took the required information from the man's driver's license, plus his phone number. After completing the transaction, he put the check in the register.

An hour later the check casher was back, this time with a knife. He proceeded to rob the store and make his escape. But he had made no attempt to alter his appearance, and the clerk had no trouble remembering him. When deputies arrived on the scene, not only was the victim able to furnish a good physical description, he also handed over the check with the man's complete identification information.

Needless to say, when the bad guy made it home he was shocked to find the deputies already there waiting for him.

DUMB CRIMINAL QUIZ NO. 602

How well do you know the dumb criminal mind?

In Concepción, Peru, townspeople were recently shocked when a man was accused of stealing two chickens. Was it because:

a) The same man had been arrested only an hour earlier for the same crime?
b) There was only one chicken living in Concepción at the time?
c) It was the first reported crime since 1762?
d) Stealing a chicken is a capital offense in Peru?

Did we fool you? The correct answer is (c). The last reported crime in Concepción, Peru, had occurred way back in 1762, when a man was charged with stealing a horse. This is a town where the Maytag repairman doubles as the sheriff.

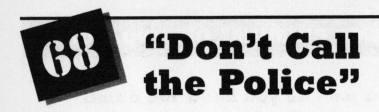

"Don't Call the Police"

Officer Timothy Walker of the Birmingham (Alabama) Task Force let America's Dumbest Criminals in on one of his personal favorites:

"I was working the eleven-to-seven shift at the time. After running a few errands that morning, I got home around one in the afternoon and went in to get some sleep. I'm lying there on the bed about half-asleep when I hear the sound of glass breaking in the living room.

"I sleep with my gun right next to the bed, so it was already in my hand as I cautiously slipped down the hallway. I heard more glass break as I spun around the corner. I'm just five feet from the window when I see the top of this head and shoulders comin' in. By the time he gets his hands on the floor and looks up, he's staring right down the barrel of my loaded .38.

"He went cross-eyed for a moment. Then I reached out and grabbed him by the shirt with my free hand, and in one swift pull I dragged him into the house."

"Don't shoot me! Please don't shoot me!" the burglar cried, perhaps remembering that old adage that says if you shoot somebody on your property, you'd better drag 'em into the house.

"I'm not going to shoot you," Walker told the frightened man, "but you're damned lucky that I didn't!"

"Don't call the police," the man pleaded. "Please don't call the police."

Walker just stared at him. The brilliant break-in artist obviously hadn't noticed the framed photos of Walker in uniform placed on a nearby table . . . or Walker's police cap in a chair . . . or the police badge on his belt . . . or the police-issue firearm nestled in Walker's hand.

"Man, look around," Walker said. "I *am* the police!"

"My Life Is Over"

Officer Gordon Martines of the Las Vegas (Nevada) Police Department was running radar one afternoon when he clocked a car at fifty miles per hour in a thirty-five zone. After Martines pulled the car over, the driver got out and walked back to the officer waving his hands in frustration. "My life is over!" the man sighed.

Martines responded, "Well, you were only doing fifteen over the limit. I wouldn't consider that life threatening at this time. May I see your driver's license, please?"

"It's been suspended," the man said.

"Then may I see your vehicle registration?"

"The car is stolen."

"All right, then. Do the license plates belong to the car?"

"The tags are stolen."

"Well, let me see if I've got this straight," Martines said, writing the ticket. "You're speeding on a revoked driver's license, the car is stolen, the tags are stolen, and you have no registration or insurance. I'm going to have to agree with you. Your life *is* over."

Funky Footwork

Pensacola, Florida, police officer Marsha Edwards was dispatched along with another marked unit to respond to a disturbance call one afternoon in a usually quiet neighborhood. The officers arrived at the location and were walking up to the door when a man came out brandishing a pistol. The officers scattered across the yard looking for the nearest cover. They drew their weapons and ordered the guy to drop his gun and lie down on the ground—which he did.

"There's three guys still fighting upstairs," he told the officers. So Officer Edwards and two other cops cautiously entered the home while a fourth officer handled the man in the yard.

As soon as they got through the door, they heard scuffling and shouts coming from upstairs. They quickly ran up the steps and found three men punching and kicking each other in a writhing heap on the floor.

Officer Edwards grabbed the first man she could get

her hands on. "I wrestled him to the ground and placed my foot on him between his shoulder and neck and told him to stay put." Meanwhile, the other cops were trying to break up the fight between the other two men.

"Lady, please," the man on the ground pleaded.

"Be quiet and stay still," Edwards told him sternly.

"But lady—"

"Just shut up and lie there," she countered, her foot still pressing down on him.

"Oh, lady, lady, please—"

"*What?*" she finally shouted at the man. "What do you want?"

"You've got dog poop all over the bottom of your shoe!"

The officer lifted her foot. "Ooooh, you're right. Sorry about that. I must've picked it up out in the front yard. Man, that's nasty."

"That's what I've been trying to tell you," he moaned.

All four men were then arrested for disturbing the peace. For the poor guy on the floor, it turned out to be a pretty crappy day all the way around.

The Couple Who Speeds Together . . .

Deputy Sheriff George Korthas of the Oswego County Sheriff's Department in the state of New York knows there are times when honesty is not always the best policy, particularly when it comes to exceeding the speed limit.

Working a radar detail one afternoon, he stopped a woman driver who was doing forty-six in a thirty-mile-per-hour zone. As the woman's car came to a halt, Deputy Korthas noticed another one pull in behind his patrol car. The male driver jumped out and hurried over to Korthas.

"Why are you stopping us?" he asked.

"I'm not stopping *you*," Korthas said. "I'm stopping the woman in this other car."

"I understand that, but we're traveling together, and I'm sure we were going the same speed."

Korthas told the man to stay by his auto while he

talked to the woman. She told him that the man in the second car was her husband and that they were indeed traveling together.

As it turned out, Deputy Korthas had clocked only the first car on radar and didn't have any proof that the second vehicle had been exceeding the speed limit. But always willing to listen to both sides, he walked back to the man standing impatiently beside his car.

Korthas told the guy he had stopped his wife for speeding but had not gotten a radar reading on his car. "Are you *sure* you were traveling the same speed as your wife?"

Clearly irritated, the man said, "Of course, I'm sure. I was right behind her. We were definitely traveling at the exact same speed."

"And what was that speed?" Korthas asked. Becoming more exasperated by the minute, the man threw up his hands and said, "I don't know, probably forty-five, maybe fifty."

Korthas said it took only a few minutes longer to write two tickets instead of one.

Otis Takes a Shortcut

Officer Brad Burris of the Pensacola (Florida) Police Department once answered a drunk-driver call at a local go-go club late one night, only to find the driver still in the parking lot—sort of. The way the club parking lot was designed, you could see the interstate below, but you had to drive out of the lot and down to the road to get there. Otherwise, there was an eight- to ten-foot drop-off.

When Burris pulled up in his cruiser, he saw that the two front wheels of the drunk's car were hanging in midair over the edge of the parking lot. He had gotten stuck trying to take a shortcut. The rear end of the car was still on the pavement, the back tires still running at about sixty miles per hour producing clouds of blue smoke.

"I walked up to the driver's-side window, and there behind the wheel was a man who looked just like Otis Campbell from *The Andy Griffith Show*," Burris says. "He was steering with both hands on the wheel and was, for all he knew, driving down the highway. His arms were rockin' a little, and he was staring intensely out the windshield. I mean, this guy was drivin'!"

Burris knocked on the window. The man gave a quick look to his left and went back to his driving, then jerked his head back left and jumped up out of his seat.

"Hey! What the . . . ?" he shouted, wide-eyed and bewildered, as if he couldn't understand how someone without a car could be running alongside him while he cruised down the highway.

"Pull over," Burris told him. The drunken man blinked widely and complied. He shut off the engine.

"Was I speeding, officer?" the man slobbered.

"Probably. Step out of the car, please."

It was all Burris could do to keep from laughing. "This guy was so drunk that he still didn't get it. As it turned out, he was a really nice guy; he'd just had too much to drink that night. Way too much." He was arrested for D.U.I.

The Draped Crusader

73

This in from Detective B. A. Treadaway of Birmingham, Alabama:

"It was a wild night! We were serving a warrant on a man at this house, and there were several people in the home at the time of the arrest. As soon as we entered, we could smell drugs. They'd been smoking pot and crack and God knows what else. We arrested the man and his friends.

"So we've got this guy handcuffed, and we're reading him his rights when he just takes off running toward the window. Now, this is a big guy, and he's flyin' on something, and he hits that window full force with his hands cuffed behind him. Clears the window out. I mean he shattered the wood, he shattered the glass. He even took the curtain with him—it was flapping in the air."

What our fool had forgotten was that the house was built on a hill, and the particular window he was in the process of jumping out of was two stories off the ground.

Treadaway and crew went running over to the window, sure that the cuffed crusader had just made his final curtain call.

"He's dead," said one of the officers, looking at the ground below.

"I was about to agree with him when this guy gets an adrenaline shot," Treadaway says. "I mean, something must've kicked in, because he jumped straight up and took off running again. Unbelievable. So the chase was on. We all scrambled outside and went running after him. I was thinking to myself, *What if we catch this guy?*"

So Treadaway and his cohorts took off in hot pursuit of the fugitive, who apparently was unaware that he was running straight toward a ten-foot drop-off. This guy didn't slow down a step. Off the ledge he went, with the curtain still flowing like a cape. And as if matters weren't already bad enough, there was a tall tree standing near the edge of the drop-off.

Crash! Our man hit the tree and snapped off a limb. *Thud!* He hit the ground and lay still.

"He's dead now," one of the officers said. But to the officers' amazement, the guy started to get up again as they moved in on him. "I'm not going to run anymore," he said.

"*Well, that's fine with me,* I thought," says Treadaway. "So we walked him back to the house, where a crowd of about ten people had gathered in the front yard, with more in the street. Some were cheering, some were booing. The cheers were for him. His buddies were all talkin' trash and trying to stir something up."

"They pushed him out the window!" one of them yelled, pointing to the vacant frame. "Yeah, I saw it all, the cops threw him out that window up there."

But before the officers could even respond, the caped crusader spoke. "No, they didn't! I jumped out the window myself," he told the mob. "They didn't push me out."

After his head started to clear up, this guy was so thankful to be alive that he even apologized to the officers for running away and causing so much trouble.

Through a Glass Dumbly

The Picture Window Flasher was notorious in Pensacola, Florida. He'd skulk around one of the numerous apartment buildings in town until he found a target he liked, then he'd expose himself through the window. Despite the fact that he left numerous fingerprints (and other smudges) on the windows, he had always managed to elude capture.

Detective Chuck Hughes, then a rookie, spotted Flasher one summer night behind an apartment complex. Hughes called for backup, and Flasher was soon apprehended. He was wearing nothing but a house key on a chain around his neck.

"Please take me by my house first," he begged as they were about to take him downtown. "I don't want to go to jail in the nude!"

The officers were kind enough to oblige him, and he was dumb enough to oblige them with another crime to charge. When they opened the front door to his house, they found a large mirror strewn with razor blades and a big pile of cocaine.

Will the Last Person to Steal the Truck Please Turn off the Lights?

75

It had been snowing in Birmingham, Alabama, for a couple of days—a rare experience for that southern city. Officer Eric Griffin and his partner were patrolling near the railroad tracks by the switching station. It was pretty well deserted except for a couple of railroad workers sitting in a utility truck.

"They must've been doing some kind of maintenance work, because the two yellow bi-lights on the top of the truck were on," Griffin says.

The officers drove past the men and proceeded to the end of the road, where they then turned around. As they were heading back they came upon the two workers, now on foot. But there was no sign of the truck.

"They just stole my truck!" one of the men shouted.

"Who stole your truck?" the officers asked.

"Two men. We were checking for loose rails, and when I looked up there were these two guys gettin' into the truck, and they just took off! It's a blue Chevy pickup with the yellow lights on top. They hit the main road and went east toward town."

The two officers dropped the two men off at the brakeman's shack and rolled. As they got into town, they passed a housing project on their right.

"There they are!" Griffin's partner suddenly yelled. Griffin looked over. Sure enough, there was the truck, with the yellow bi-lights still flashing away. The officers turned into the projects and had to make several twists and turns in order to get over to where they'd seen the lights. When they got there, the truck was gone. But then Griffin's partner spotted it again. "There they go, the next street over!"

As the officers turned at the next street, the truck passed directly in front of them. The bi-lights were still flashing. One of the men was kicking frantically on the dash and holding a fistful of wires. He still hadn't found the off switch. Finally, with the help of another unit, Griffin and company were able to trap the vehicle and make the arrest.

"As we were taking the passenger out of the truck, I couldn't help myself," Griffin recalls. "I reached in and turned off the lights."

One of the men was kicking frantically on the dash and holding a fistful of wires.

The Car Dealer, the Card Dealer, and Mom

One crazy story told by Officer Bruce Harper and still making the rounds among Las Vegas, Nevada, police officers concerns two brothers and their seventy-year-old mother who stopped by a car dealership in Las Vegas. They asked the salesman if they could test-drive a particular new car. He threw a set of tags on it, climbed in the backseat, and they were off.

After they'd gone a few miles, one of the men asked his brother to pull over so he could drive the car. When they stopped, they ordered the salesman out of the backseat and forced him into the trunk. Then they shut the lid and headed out of town.

Another motorist had witnessed the entire event. He followed them to a casino outside of Vegas and phoned the police. The officers arrived and freed the shaken salesman, who was able to give them a good description of his unlikely kidnappers.

The officers couldn't be sure just how many people might actually be involved, so they acted with caution. A S.W.A.T. team was dispatched to the scene. The team entered the casino and went directly to the security room filled with closed-circuit television monitors. Moments later they spotted one of the brothers seated at a black-jack table.

To apprehend him and the rest of his family, several members of the S.W.A.T. team dressed up like waiters and carried towels and drink trays concealing their weapons. Three of the disguised officers came up behind the brother who had been spotted. Surrounding the guy, they pulled him straight back off his chair and onto the floor. No one else at the table looked up. They were too interested in their card game to care about anything else, but that's Vegas.

Meanwhile, other members of the team had located and arrested the remaining brother. With both brothers now in custody, the focus was on Mom. They'd gotten her name from her sons, so catching her was simply a matter of paging her on the casino intercom system.

The three were charged with grand theft auto and kidnapping. Why an entire family would kidnap a total stranger, put him into the trunk, and then stop to gamble is beyond logic. But then, these weren't exactly the Waltons.

Out of the Frying Pan, into the Line of Fire

It was a moonless, balmy Pensacola, Florida, night, and there he was—a criminal fleeing on foot and feeling pretty good about his chances of making the next street and therefore slipping into the anonymous darkness.

Suddenly, behind him, came the screech of tires and the unmistakable flash of a police cruiser's lights. What to do? He knew the neighborhood well, having cased most of the houses during his career.

The next house on the left, he thought. *It's just that little old lady living alone. I'll bust in there. She won't be hard to deal with. After the heat's off, I'll help myself to her jewelry box and get out.*

He ran to the front porch and heaved himself against the front door. No luck. Again he rammed the door with his shoulder. Again it didn't budge. A step back, a swift kick, and the door finally flew open. He slipped inside the door and closed it.

Did they see me? If they did, I'll just take the old bag hostage.

From the darkened hallway came the distinctive sound of a twelve-gauge, pump-action shotgun being readied for use. A southern lady's delicate voice rose quite calmly from the shadows: "You might have better luck with those policemen outside, young man. If you move anywhere but out that door, I'll just have to blow your head off."

The patrolmen who had seen the idiot burglar-to-be enter the house reported that his exit was much faster and that he seemed rather relieved to see three policemen there to save him.

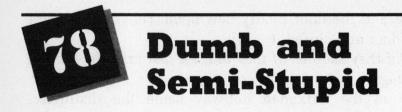

Dumb and Semi-Stupid

Veteran female police officer Alson Dula told America's Dumbest Criminals this story about a man who, by any known standard, just has to be one of, well, one of America's dumbest criminals.

Officer Dula was on patrol in the lovely and historic town of Davidson, North Carolina, when she noticed that the man who just passed her had expired plates on his car. She hit the lights and with a quick blip of the siren pulled him over.

Dula ran the tag number. Not only were the tags expired, but they also didn't belong to the car. The man's driver's license had been revoked as well. She arrested him on those charges.

Exactly one month later to the day, the same man drove through town. Same car. Same tags. Same revoked license. Same officer. He was arrested on the same charges. He again went to jail, made bond, and was awaiting trial when one month later he decided to rob a department store.

He held a knife in his right hand and a newspaper in his left as he approached the counter, putting the newspaper in front of his face as he asked the clerk to hand over all the money in her drawer. She couldn't see his face, but then he had no way of noticing that the clerk was writing down the company name stitched on the blue work shirt the man was wearing, along with his name—which happened to be spelled out above his pocket. You know what comes next: He was found guilty of armed robbery and sentenced to prison.

One month later this guy broke out of jail at night and stole a Mack tractor-trailer truck, minus the trailer. Now he was a free man, so where did he go? Back to town, of course. The police spotted him in the stolen truck, and the chase was on. He was running from one county to another in that Mack truck and soon he had ten cop cars lined up behind him.

Eventually, he decided to drive by the trailer park where his mom lived. She was looking out her trailer window when she saw him go by, still honking the air horn with the squad cars in his wake. "Look, Ma, no brains!"

From there he drove over to the next county, where he and his wife lived in another trailer park. Doing about forty miles an hour, he drove the stolen Mack truck across his front yard and slammed the semi into the front door of his trailer. Then he jumped out of the truck and ran inside.

"Honey, I'm home!" She wasn't. His wife had been informed of his escape and had gone to stay in the neighbor's trailer, from where she watched the whole thing in numb horror.

Police were everywhere—local, state, and county. They surrounded the mobile home and cut off the power to his trailer. Approximately forty-five minutes later, our dumbbell cracked. He walked out of what was left of his trailer with his hands up and surrendered to the anxiously awaiting police. He is now serving his old and new sentences in the penitentiary.

Originality Counts

According to Charlotte, North Carolina, patrolman T. C. Owen, a man trying to explain the presence of his fingerprints at several different crime scenes insisted that "someone has been going around town, using my fingerprints."

High-Tech Bomb Threat

It's entirely possible for even high-tech bad guys to be dumb criminals—as in the case of the Florida teenager who decided to use a fax machine to make a bomb threat to his high school.

Although it might have been a stupid idea—even *he* knew that the phone number of the originating fax machine is automatically printed on the fax—this young genius wasn't about to use his own machine. His unbeatable idea would be to use another fax machine and a toll-free number that he had been told could not be traced.

He called a large computer company and asked the person answering for technical assistance. One of the services the company provided was a computer faxing service. The customer could type in a fax number, and the information would be automatically transmitted to that number. Of course, the customer was also expected to put his name on the message. But the kid was too smart for that. In the message box intended for the sender's name, he typed a long message about a bomb being in the high school, along with a few other threats. He then typed in the fax number of his high school, transmitted the message, and quickly disconnected. Immensely pleased with himself, he sat back to see what sort of chaos would transpire.

Unbeknownst to the young man, most of his message was lost in transmission. Because the name box accepts a total of only twenty characters (including spaces), all that went through were the words, "There is a bomb in—"

The school authorities called the cops and, when they arrived, turned over the fax. Lo and behold, it contained the toll-free number of the computer company's technical support line. From there, it was a simple matter for the company to check its records and find where the call had originated.

Within a half-hour the young prankster was in custody. In the presence of his parents, he was soon confessing all and was eventually charged with making the bomb threat. Sadder but wiser after being expelled, the young computer whiz learned that a little knowledge can indeed be a dangerous thing.

Buried Treasure

Retired Escambia County (Florida) Sheriff's Department captain Don Parker knows that modern-day pirates still sometimes bury their loot in the sand. He has some firsthand experience in the matter.

It happened on a quiet summer's night on Pensacola Beach, as Parker and reserve deputy David Stanley were patrolling in Parker's unmarked car. Traffic was light, and there were plenty of tourists and locals walking around enjoying the balmy evening breezes.

As they approached a stop sign, Parker noticed a car behind them in the other lane and coming up fast. To his surprise, the vehicle, a rusted and battered four-door sedan, shot through the intersection, ignoring the stop sign. Unfortunately, a Volkswagen bug was in the wrong place at the wrong time, and the larger car broadsided the VW, spinning it around like a top.

"Luckily, there were no injuries," Parker says, "but it all happened so fast we didn't have time to react."

After the sounds of breaking glass and screeching tires subsided, the two officers jumped out to render aid. Then a strange thing happened.

"The guy sitting on the passenger side of the big sedan came out of the car like a jack-in-a-box, ran to the side of the road, and began digging a small hole," Parker recalls. "David and I watched in amazement as he pulled two sandwich bags full of marijuana from his pocket, dropped them in the hole, and quickly covered the dope with sand.

"Now, it's true we were driving a plain car, but both of us were in full uniform and no more than ten feet from where the man was digging in the sand. Apparently, though, he didn't see us."

Satisfied that the damning evidence had been successfully hidden, the guy casually strolled back to the accident scene. Parker told Stanley to go and stand on the spot where the dope had been buried. Then he went to direct traffic until a trooper could arrive to work the wreck.

A highway patrolman was soon on the scene, and the driver of the sedan freely admitted that he had run the stop sign. Both he and his passenger were friendly and cooperative, and the investigation was quickly completed. The trooper wrote a citation to the at-fault driver, then closed his notebook. "Well," he said to Parker, "I guess that does it."

He pulled two sandwich bags full of marijuana from his pocket, dropped them in the hole, and quickly covered the dope with sand.

Parker smiled. "Not quite." He nodded at Stanley, who quickly dug up the two little bags and held them up for everyone to see. "We found some buried treasure, and I think we know who buried it."

The two dumb (and dumbfounded) criminals were quickly handcuffed and placed in the back of Parker's car for the short trip to the beach jail.

A Self-Inflicted Drive-By

Drive-by shootings are the scourge of lower-income neighborhoods. Gangs use this cowardly and costly practice to retaliate against enemies and rival gangs—with deadly effect on innocent children and adults who just happen to be in the wrong place at the wrong time. Drive-bys also escalate the cycle of violence as one act of revenge replaces another. But we did hear of a drive-by shooting in Oklahoma that ended with some poetic justice for a change.

A carload of gang members had set out to avenge their honor by taking a few potshots at their rivals on a city street. Their car was a "low rider" loaded down with six young gang members. They cruised the dark night streets, patrolling their "turf" and searching for some stragglers from another gang.

Finally, they spotted their prey—three kids walking

and apparently not aware of the car behind them. The setup was perfect. Nobody else was on the street. All was quiet, no stores were open, and no cops were anywhere to be seen. The cruising shooters cut off their headlights, killed the radio, and silently idled up the street, barely moving.

Just as the shooter in the backseat was ready to pull the trigger, the car's front right wheel rolled into a huge pothole. The car bounced, the gun fired, the front left tire blew, and the young men on the sidewalk scattered. The driver gunned the engine and rode the rim for about half a block; then the wheel came off the axle and the car screeched to a grating stop. The gunman inside the car had foolishly shot out his own tire.

When the police arrived to apprehend the gang members, they found them arguing and fighting amongst themselves over the flat tire.

No Fair

Detective John Crain of Birmingham, Alabama, and his partner were working undercover, doing drug buys and arresting prostitutes. One night they happened to be down by the state fairgrounds, when a citizen flagged them down.

"I been seein' y'all out here cruisin' around," the man said. "Guess you must be workin' at the fair. I just wanted to let y'all know that I can get you anything you want. Anything! I can get you drugs, prostitutes, housing—you name it. I'm the man to see."

Not wanting to pass up a good opportunity, Crain asked the man, "Can you get us some crack?"

"No problem, man; just run me down the street here."

So Crain and his partner gave him a lift to a certain house, where he went in to get the drugs. Then he said, "Hey, I've got two women in my motel room. Let's go over there and do some partyin'."

"So we take this guy over to this sleazy motel and go

into the room," Crain says. "But instead of two women waiting there, we met three more men."

This changed everything. Suddenly, the odds were four to two, and the officers had no backup. Crain and his partner didn't know if this was a setup or how many of these guys had weapons or what. So they just continued to play along.

"Hey, let's smoke some of that rock you just got," one of the men finally said to Crain.

"I want to wait for the girls," Crain coolly answered. "We'll smoke it when they get here, and then we'll go get some more."

"We don't have to go get more," one of the others said. "We've got plenty right here."

At that point, everybody started pulling out rocks of cocaine. They were arguing with each other about who had the best stuff. It was definitely time to end the party.

"Police officers!" Crain yelled. "Everybody freeze!"

"This was a tense situation," Crain remembers. "At any moment, one of them could have pulled a gun and started shooting. I'm thinkin', *We need some backup,* but I didn't know how we could call for backup without the means to do so. It was a standoff for a minute. Then I took hold of my collar and began talking into one of the buttons on my lapel."

"Hold your positions; we are in control!" Crain barked

"Hold your positions; we are in control!" Crain barked into his, uh, microphone.

into his, uh, microphone. "All units, hold your positions!"

While this charade was going on, Crain's partner managed to slip out of the room and call for real backup. All of the men were arrested.

Says Crain, "The one who thought we worked at the fair asked me later, 'What was that button you were talkin' into? Man, you guys are comin' up with some neat stuff nowadays.'

"*Yeah,* I thought, *we sure are.*"

When You're Right, You're Right

Traffic violations tend to stimulate creativity, engendering some of the most original excuses ever thought of, and all cops have their favorites. Former Baltimore, Maryland, police officer Frank Walmer remembers one of the best excuses he ever heard.

"I was dispatched to handle a traffic accident at the corner of Mulberry and Carey," he says. "When I got there I found five bent and battered cars but no serious injuries. Of course, things were pretty confused, with angry drivers milling around, a big crowd of people, and a major traffic snarl."

Walmer set to work trying to untangle the situation, but the job took quite awhile. "After awhile I noticed a man standing off to one side, wearing a tuxedo. As I walked over to talk to him, several of the drivers said that he was the one who had caused the wreck by running a red light."

Ignoring the shouted accusations, the man readily

responded to Walmer's request for a driver's license. He handed it to him with a smile and said, "These people are wrong. I was not at fault."

Walmer told him that at least a half-dozen witnesses had accused him of running the red light.

The man nodded. "Yes, it's true I ran the red light, but I had the right of way."

Officer Walmer asked him how that could be true. He didn't appear to have been driving an emergency vehicle, and that would have been the only way he could claim the right of way in such a situation.

The driver smoothed the lapels of his tuxedo, looked disdainfully at the shouting rabble, then said loftily, "Of course, I had the right of way. I was in a wedding procession."

A Bad Hair Day

Officer Bill Cromie of the Oswego County (New York) Sheriff's Department has heard his share of excuses from traffic violators, but one in particular sticks in his mind.

On a warm summer afternoon he was working a traffic detail when he saw a car approaching at a pretty good clip.

"There was a young man driving, and I was struck by the fact that he was driving with his head hanging out the window like a cocker spaniel," Cromie said. "He was also doing sixty-five in a thirty according to my radar, but he stopped right away when I turned on my lights.

"I walked up to the driver's side and noticed that the man's hair was dripping wet. I asked him if there was some kind of medical emergency, but he said there wasn't."

It turned out the young man was on his way to his girl-friend's house and had just washed his hair. Unfortunately, his hair dryer was broken. "I just hate to go over there with wet hair," he said. "So I figured I would just stick my head out the window and let the wind do it for me. I guess I wasn't watching my speed."

Cromie said it was one of the most original excuses he had ever heard, so he let the young man off with a warning. As he was walking back to his patrol car, the now-happy man yelled his thanks, then added, "And I promise I'll get a new hair dryer."

86 O, Please

Las Vegas, Nevada, policeman Sam Hilliard and his partner were on routine red-eye patrol at about three o'clock one morning when they were flagged down by a concerned citizen about a disturbance that was keeping him—and the whole neighborhood—awake. It seems that farther down the street there was a strange man throwing rocks at the neighborhood church and cursing loudly.

After hearing the concerned citizen's story, the officer who was driving stepped on the gas and headed to the church, where he and his partner found a man fitting the citizen's description of the suspect. The officers pulled up alongside the man and asked, "Were you the one throwing rocks at the church?"

"Yes, I was. So what?"

"So why were you doing that?"

"I'm mad at the church!"

"Why are you mad at the church?"

The man launched into a brief explanation having something to do with the church not having a picture of Jesus Christ dying on the cross. And that apparently had made the man angry enough to cast stones.

By this time, the officers had managed to get a good whiff of the rock thrower. It was clear he had been drinking—a lot. The officers weren't about to get into a religious discussion with a drunk, but they felt compelled to exit their cruiser and investigate more closely. After all, this was a public place, and there had been a disturbance.

"We began patting the man down," one of the cops remembers. "Reaching into a large inside jacket pocket, we pulled out this big letter *O*. Of course, we asked him what it was."

"That's my *O*," he replied.

"Your *O*?"

"Yeah, that's my souvenir from the church."

The two officers looked up at the front of the church. Sure enough, the word *Catholic* in the church's main sign was missing its *O*. Told that the *O* rightfully belonged to the church, the man reluctantly consented to giving it back to the officers. They thanked him and told him to be on his way, but not to do any driving.

"After the man left, we returned the big *O* to its place and were in the process of writing the resident priest a note explaining what had happened when this car comes slowly rolling up."

Guess who!

The officers didn't know what to expect. Maybe the guy now had a gun on him. Maybe he had revenge on his mind. No matter. The two officers quickly drew their weapons and ordered the man to stop the car and get out.

"I want my *O*!" the man ranted and raved. "Give me my *O*! It's my *O*!"

It eventually dawned on the officers that the man wasn't armed. But he was still drunk. So they had little resistance when it came to making the arrest.

"Enough was enough," our Vegas friends told America's Dumbest Criminals. "We tried to give him a break the first time, figuring that his anger was between him and God. But when he became a drunk driver, that was between him and us.

"And, *'O'* yeah, we arrested him for D.U.I."

Sprechen Sie Deutsch?

Officer Arnold Hagman of the Boise (Idaho) Police Department was born in Germany and speaks fluent German. Working a traffic detail one day, he stopped a woman for speeding. When he walked up to the car to obtain her driver's license, she gave him a helpless, melting smile and said, in German, that she didn't speak any English.

Officer Hagman was more than just sympathetic. Nodding politely, he said, *"Heute ist ein glücklicher Tag für Sie,"* which means, of course, This is your lucky day.

Evidently, she disagreed, because the smile disappeared much faster than it had appeared.

Going Down

Sgt. Ernest Burt of the Birmingham (Alabama) Police Department has served hundreds of arrest warrants in his time. But few have involved cases as bizarre as this one, the moral of which suggests that a criminal's guilt can bear a heavy burden.

One morning, officers approached the door to one of the units in one of Birmingham's oldest apartment buildings and began knocking. They stood there for several minutes patiently rapping away, waiting for a response. Finally, an elderly woman opened the door a crack, revealing a dour expression and saying nothing.

"We have an arrest warrant for a Mrs. Sheryl Tary," Burt said. "Is she at home?"

"No, she's not here," the woman curtly answered.

Burt pressed on, politely telling the woman at the door that he and his partner would like to come in and look around. He was in the process of explaining himself to the uncooperative greeter when, suddenly, they heard a tremendous crashing sound from a room inside.

"I mean it was *loud,*" Burt said. "My partner and I quickly looked at each other, pushed open the front door, and rushed inside to see what had happened. When we got to the living room, we couldn't believe our eyes."

There, lying on the ground groaning, was a woman weighing about three hundred pounds, surrounded by and covered with pieces of plaster, some of which were still fluttering to the floor. She had fallen through the ceiling from the attic, where she had been hiding out.

Sheryl Tary, we presume.

"We told her to just lie still," said Burt, who by this time was biting his lip. "We dispatched an ambulance to the scene. Three paramedics carried her off on a gurney. At the time, her condition was quite serious, but after they told us she would be all right, we just had to laugh. I'll bet even *she* laughed about it later."

How well do you know the dumb criminal mind?

What was the greatest number of people ever arrested at one time in a democratic nation? Was it:

a) 806?
b) 421?
c) 1,201?
d) 308?
e) 15,617?

The answer is (e). On July 11, 1988, police in South Korea rounded up and arrested 15,617 demonstrators in one form or fashion protesting that summer's Olympic games in Seoul—before the games had even begun!

A Real Drunk Driver

89

A California police officer told us about the time he was especially worried about the car weaving in front of him. It was nighttime, and the road was not well lit. The driver obviously was having a difficult time staying in his lane. He would drift over the double yellow line to his left, then edge over almost to the ditch on his right. The officer had been behind him for nearly a mile with lights flashing and siren wailing when the man finally made a crude stop on the side of the road. He slumped forward onto the steering wheel as the officer approached his car.

"Sir," the officer said, tapping on the driver's window with his flashlight, "turn the car off for me, and step out of the vehicle, please."

The man was dangerously drunk. As he got out of the car, he staggered back against the fender and slid nearly to the ground. The officer kept him from falling.

"I haven't dren binking, occifer," the man slurred.

"How much have you had to drink tonight, sir?" the officer asked.

"I haven't dren binking, occifer," the man slurred.

"Lying to me isn't going to help you, sir. Now, how much have you had to drink?"

"A couple uh beers," he muttered. "Zat's all."

"A couple of beers? Do you take any medication, sir?"

"No. Not that I know of."

"Not that you know of? I need to see your driver's license, sir."

The man fumbled through his wallet and produced a license. As he handed it to the officer, there suddenly was a terrible crash nearby. Two cars had crashed into one another and been knocked to the side of the road.

"Wait right here!" the officer ordered the drunken man. "Don't you move!"

With that the policeman ran forward to the crash site. He was talking with the people involved in the accident when he suddenly saw the drunk man driving past him at a high rate of speed. "Hey!" the officer yelled at him as the man sped by.

Thirty minutes later the police were at the man's house and had it surrounded. Six or seven squad cars sat out in front, and several officers with guns drawn were positioning themselves around the front yard. They were pounding on the door and shouting, "Police! Open up!"

A still-drunk and very groggy man finally answered the door and was immediately seized by the officers, handcuffed, and arrested.

"Hey, what the hell is goin' on here?" he asked belligerently.

"Where's the car?" the officers demanded to know.

"The what?" he asked. "I've been home all night sleeping."

"Where is the car?"

"It's in the garage, I guess. That's where I usually park it." The man seemed totally befuddled.

"Here it is!" an officer shouted from the now-opened garage.

Sure enough, there it sat. The garage was filled with exhaust fumes. The engine was still running. So were the blue lights on the top of the squad car. The guy was so drunk he hadn't even realized that he'd driven off in the police cruiser instead of his own car.

Never Talk to Strangers

Retired police captain Don Parker told America's Dumbest Criminals about a man named Simon Bolivar McElroy. He was having a bad day. After being freed from a Florida jail, where he had served time for a drug conviction, McElroy was on his way to catch a little sun at the beach. More to the point, he was going there to sell four plastic sandwich bags of marijuana. But en route to the beach, McElroy heard a metallic *clunk* when he hit the gas after stopping for a traffic light. The engine in his rusty old van had died.

McElroy grabbed his cigarettes and his lighter, shoved the bags of marijuana down inside his underwear, and walked away from the van, leaving the keys dangling from the ignition. McElroy stuck out his thumb and quickly caught a ride. Although he would miss the van, he didn't want to be anywhere near it when the cops showed up.

His ride took him all the way to the beach. He was

beginning to feel better as he sat on the sand enjoying the warm breezes and the passing bikinis. The bags were making him itch, though, so he transferred them to his front pockets and started walking down the beach, looking for potential customers.

McElroy had just topped a sand dune next to a big hotel when he stopped dead in his tracks. Spread out in front of him were at least a hundred guys who looked just like him, with scraggly beards, long, stringy hair, and pasty-white bodies. They were lying on blankets, throwing Frisbees, or splashing in the surf. It looked like a druggie's family reunion.

He walked over to a couple of likely prospects and casually asked if they'd be interested in purchasing some weed. They not only were interested, but they also wanted to buy his entire supply! They dickered over the price and finally settled on an amount at least three times the going street price.

The guy he had been talking to called several others over, and in no time there was quite a little pile of greenbacks on the blanket beside the marijuana. McElroy started to reach for the money, but the guy stopped him. He told McElroy that they were now permanent friends and that he was going to sign his initials on every single bill as a token of his admiration for McElroy's kindness. Someone produced a pen, and the guy did exactly that.

Although McElroy thought this behavior bizarre, he wouldn't have cared if the idiot had danced an Irish jig.

When the last bill had been signed, McElroy was given the money. He was about to take his leave when the guy told him he had some bad news. Before McElroy could react, each of the long-haired spectators suddenly produced a badge. They were of all shapes and colors and represented a variety of local, state, and federal law enforcement agencies.

As he was being escorted to the hotel to await the arrival of a uniformed patrol officer, McElroy was told he had managed to find an entire convention of narcotics investigators, in town to attend a training seminar.

The guy who had marked the bills was one of the instructors. He slapped McElroy on the back and told him to cheer up. "Look on the bright side," he said. "At least we'll have a really great story to start off tomorrow's session."

That Volunteer Spirit

Officer Paul Hickman and two other narcotics officers were searching a pair of crack dealers on a street corner in Charlotte, North Carolina. It was a bright, beautiful day. People were walking the sidewalks, taking in the air. It was the kind of afternoon when anything seemed possible.

As the officers were cuffing the crack dealers, a young man approached them and said, "Hey, do you want to search me?"

It seemed like a setup. No one would just come up out of the blue and offer to be searched if he had anything to hide. But one officer, perhaps enjoying the humor of the gesture, said, "All right" and proceeded to pat him down.

The officer found a bag of crack cocaine in the man's pocket.

"Oh, man," complained the volunteer, "I was just being polite! You weren't supposed to say yes!"

Nothing to Fear but Fear Itself

It was about ten at night when Deputy Sheriff Bill Cromie of Oswego County, New York, was dispatched to a traffic accident in the small town of Constantia, New York. Arriving on the scene, he found that a car had crashed into some gasoline pumps and that the intoxicated driver had fled the scene on foot. The rescue squad had foamed the whole area down to prevent a fire, and things seemed to be under control.

Cromie asked if anyone had any idea which direction the missing driver had run. One of the firefighters pointed toward a ravine next to the road. "He ran down there," he said. "He's been crashing around in the woods for the last hour. You can still hear him."

Sure enough, the sounds of something large and clumsy barreling through the foliage, could be plainly heard. The ravine was pitch dark, and Cromie proceeded cautiously down the steep slope, heading toward the sound of snapping branches. As he got closer he could also hear heavy breathing.

He turned on his flashlight. There, illuminated by the beam, was one pitiful human being. Filthy, scraped and scratched, his clothing in tatters and utterly exhausted, the still-drunk driver blinked in the glare.

"Sheriff's Department," Cromie announced. "Are you the driver of that car back there?"

The man slid to the ground, panting heavily, and raised his trembling hands. "I give up," he said. "I was driving, and I thought I could get away through the woods." He shook his head wearily. "You must be Superman."

Cromie asked him what he meant. "Man, you been chasing me for forty-five minutes, and you aren't even winded. Hell, you ain't even messed up the crease in your pants. How did you do it?"

Cromie laughed and told the man that he had only just arrived on the scene and that no one had been chasing him. The drunk let this information sink in for a few minutes, then looked up. "You mean I been chasing myself?"

"I'm afraid so."

The guy struggled to his feet. "Well, if I'm that damn stupid, you might as well put me in jail." Cromie was happy to oblige.

A
Doubleheader

While on patrol during a midnight shift in Baltimore, Maryland, Officer Frank Walmer spotted a guy walking down the street carrying a television. The man made no attempt to escape as Walmer approached, and he readily furnished identification. He said the television belonged to him. He had recently lent it to a friend and now was taking it home.

"I ran the serial number and had communications check for any recent burglaries involving that brand of TV," Walmer says. "But they found nothing, so I had to let the guy go."

But just before he got off duty, Walmer was dispatched to the scene of a residential burglary and, sure enough, one of the items stolen was a television of the make and model that he had just seen on the street.

"The homeowner was really upset and was running around the living room showing me where all the missing items had been, the broken window where the burglars had gained entry, and the items that might have fingerprints. But the really interesting thing was that on the coffee table, in plain view, were at least three ounces of marijuana, a stack of rolling papers, scales, and several roach clips."

Walmer took all the information furnished by the irate homeowner and then pointed at the dope. "You say they got your television but not your marijuana, is that right?"

The guy nodded. "That's right. They came through the window, got my TV, but left the—" His voice died as he realized what he was about to say. He looked at the dope, looked at Walmer, and then swallowed hard. "I can't believe I left that stuff there," he whispered.

"As I was handcuffing him, I told him the situation wasn't all bleak, because I was pretty sure I would be able to recover his television." And Walmer did just that. Because he had the previous suspect's complete address, Walmer drove to his house and found him sitting in his living room watching the stolen TV.

"All in all," Walmer remembers, "it was a pretty good night."

One for the Road

Tampa, Florida, police officer David Shepler has won an award for arresting more drunk drivers in one year than anyone else in his department. His experience and skill stand him in good stead even when responding to routine traffic calls—like the one that took him to the scene of a traffic accident on Interstate 275 near the Tampa airport.

Arriving on the scene, Officer Shepler found a nearly demolished car up against the guardrail of the busy interstate. "The first thing I saw was about three hundred feet of red paint where the car had scraped and skidded all along the guardrail. The next thing I noticed was that the car was still moving—but barely."

Shepler ran to the car and found the driver still behind the wheel, doing his best to drive his wrecked vehicle away. "I told him to turn off the engine, but he said he was in a hurry and had to be someplace. It was then I realized he was heavily intoxicated, so I reached through the window and took the keys."

The driver staggered out of the car and stood by the door, swaying like a sapling in a strong wind. Shepler told him he suspected him of being drunk and was going to give him some roadside sobriety tests. "As soon as I told him this, the guy reached inside the car and hauled out a six-pack of beer. He pulled off two cans and offered me one. I refused it and told him again I was about to administer a roadside sobriety test."

The inebriated driver nodded and said, "Yeah, I heard all that. But I do much better on tests when I've had something to drink."

Needless to say, Officer Shepler had to inform the man that he had had quite enough to drink. The Breathalyzer reading confirmed this, reading his blood alcohol level at .31—which is more than three times the legal limit in Florida.

Watch That First Step

Working security at the Carter Center in Atlanta, Georgia, is a lot like working any other security job, except for having an ex-president of the United States as your boss. Protective Operations Director Jeff Dingle is used to handling the routine problems common to any big city operation. Every now and then, however, something truly unusual will happen. Like the case of the missing rosebushes.

The rose garden at the Carter Center is pleasing to the eye, but the plants are not inexpensive. So Jeff was understandably concerned when a groundskeeper told him that five of the plants had been stolen the previous night. The next day, five more disappeared, and five more the day after that. Because the thefts were obviously occurring after normal business hours, Dingle decided to set up surveillance on the rose garden in hopes of catching the thief.

Well aware that stakeouts can be mind numbingly

Within a few minutes he had dug up three plants while the protective operations director watched.

boring, Jeff was mentally prepared for hours of tedious monotony. For the early hours he decided he could get a good view of the garden by simply sitting on a nearby bench like any other tourist. The center closes at five o'clock in the afternoon, and by that time Dingle was on his bench hoping against hope that the rosebush thief might put in an early appearance.

He didn't have to wait long. At two minutes after five, one of the local crackheads, carrying a small shovel, came around the corner and headed straight for the roses. Within a few minutes he had dug up three plants while the protective operations director watched in amazement.

Realizing he needed to take action, Dingle walked over to the man, identified himself, and asked him what he was doing. The guy threw down the shovel, assured Dingle he wasn't doing a thing, and then turned and ran. Dingle pursued him while calling for assistance on his radio.

Now picture a building built into the side of a hill, with a back roofline only two feet off the ground. The suspect jumped up onto this low-slung roof and headed for the other side with Dingle still in pursuit. Unfortunately for this dumb rose thief, the other end of the roof is twenty-eight feet off the ground, a fact he discovered only when he reached it. He skidded to a stop and looked back to see several security people closing in.

Frantically looking around for an escape route, the thief looked to one side and saw a grassy area leading down to a small lake. Convinced that freedom lay in that direction, he did the dumbest possible thing. He jumped.

Big mistake. The grassy area and lake were some distance away. And directly below the point where he jumped was a concrete sidewalk, which is what the rose thief hit, breaking both legs.

The ensuing excitement, with police cars and an ambulance and lots of uniforms, attracted quite a crowd. As the unfortunate suspect was being loaded into the ambulance, one of the late arrivals asked what the guy had done. Told that the man had stolen a rosebush, he shook his head in amazement.

"I always heard they was tough in Atlanta," he said. "But I didn't know they was that tough!"

Those Small-Town Blues

High school graduation night is a time of celebration as one era ends and another begins. Of course, there are always those who have a tendency to overindulge. It was well past midnight when Deputy Bill Cromie of Phoenix, New York, spotted such a future leader of tomorrow driving along the shoulder of the road at fifteen miles an hour.

Cromie loaded up the intoxicated young driver and took him to jail. En route, the kid complained bitterly that Cromie had no right to arrest him because he was a Vietnam veteran who had honorably served his country. Deputy Cromie would have been impressed, except the kid's driver's license indicated he had been born two years after the Vietnam War ended!

Cromie brought the kid inside and sat him down in a chair. The lad sat quietly for a few moments as Cromie worked on his report, but then suddenly shouted, "Don't do that! Stop it! Stop hitting me!" Amused, Cromie ignored him, but the kid kept yelling and then he suddenly kicked backward, tipping over the chair and crashing to the floor. Cromie's sergeant came running and found the still-intoxicated driver lying on the floor.

"Call me an ambulance," the kid wailed pitifully.

Cromie looked up from his report and said, "All right, you're an ambulance."

Cromie then turned to the sergeant and explained what had happened, assuring him there was nothing wrong. The kid, realizing his plan wasn't working, righted the chair and sat in silence while Cromie finished the paperwork.

An hour later Cromie and his prisoner stood in front of the judge. Cromie explained the facts in the case, including the boy's attempt to fake a charge of police brutality. As Cromie finished his narrative the boy turned and snarled, "You're nothing but a small-town cop." The judge cautioned him to refrain from gratuitous insults and was promptly told that he was "nothing but a small-town judge."

The judge smiled. "You may be right, son, but I've got some good news for you. We do have a big-city jail, and you're going to get to spend some time in it."

It Seemed Like 97 a Good Idea at the Time

When William S. Meyers was with the Anne Arundel County Police Department in Maryland, he heard about a couple of less-than-intellectual giants who decided they would rob an automatic teller machine.

Of course, our crooks knew they couldn't just walk up to a machine, point a gun at it, and demand money. They knew ATMs are protected by alarms and surveillance cameras: any attempt to break into the machine would likely result in a whole bunch of cops showing up. But they were going to avoid all that because they had a fool-proof plan. They would steal the entire machine.

The scheme was simplicity itself. Late at night they would attach a chain to the ATM, then fasten the chain to the back bumper of their pickup. When everything was secure, they would hit the gas, jerk the machine right out of the wall, and be gone long before the cops arrived on the scene.

They picked a dark and rainy Friday night when the streets were deserted and the ATM was likely to have a fresh supply of money for the weekend. They quietly wrapped the chain around the machine, then tied it securely to the back bumper of their truck. The driver pushed the pedal to the floor, and the pickup shot forward.

Because the ATM appeared to be mounted securely, the would-be thieves had used a heavy chain to make sure it would stand the strain. Unfortunately for them, they had not used a heavy-duty pickup. When the chain snapped taut, it ripped the back bumper right off.

With alarm bells ringing, sirens yelping, and strobe lights flashing, the panic-stricken crooks didn't even slow down, and soon they were far away. Although shaken by the experience, they were happy to escape and even laughed at the thought of the cops arriving to find them long gone.

What they didn't realize was that when the rear bumper was torn off the license plate went with it. It didn't take long for the responding officers to obtain a registration, along with names and addresses. Within the hour, they were adding two more dumb criminals to the large selection already housed in the county jail.

You Snooze, You Lose

Detective Dennis Larsen tells us about a pair of high achievers who were fired from their jobs at a Las Vegas, Nevada, car rental agency. Disgruntled, they plotted to rob the manager. They knew the exact time and bank at which the manager made a nightly deposit. So they hatched a plan whereby one of them would lie in wait with a gun and the other would cruise the area on getaway standby.

The first conspirator (we'll call him Heckle) dropped his partner (Jeckle) at the bank about thirty minutes before the manager was due. Jeckle donned a ski mask and took his place behind a Dumpster with a commanding view of the night depository. Heckle set about inconspicuously driving around the block at three miles an hour.

Jeckle waited. Heckle drove. Jeckle got drowsy. Heckle drove. Jeckle fell asleep. The manager made his deposit. Heckle drove. Jeckle slept. Heckle drove.

Police responded to a report of a man sleeping in a ski mask behind a Dumpster and a car out of gas nearby.

K-911

After filling his tank at a Denver, Colorado, gas station, Jeff King decided to rob the station attendant. As King jumped into his car to make his getaway, his one-year-old puppy jumped out to relieve himself. King made several unsuccessful attempts to coax the animal back into the car but eventually was forced to abandon his beloved pet. He knew that, by now, the police were surely on their way.

Within moments of the cops' arrival, the playful pup had become perfectly content to stand still while the officers scratched his ears and read his dogtag, complete with the owner's name and address.

Let's see, if seven years of a dog life equals one human year, the dog should be about fifty when his master gets out of prison.

Only a Phone Call Away

As a school resource officer in Tampa, Florida, David Shepler one day was called in to handle a locker theft. A teenage girl reported that twenty dollars and a pager had been stolen from her locker.

School authorities had a suspect, another teenage girl. Officer Shepler questioned her about the theft. She eventually admitted that she had taken the twenty dollars (which she returned) but stoutly denied taking the pager.

After several minutes of fruitless questioning, Shepler told the victim to go to a nearby phone and dial the pager's number. She did as requested. A moment later a strange beeping and clattering sound came from where the suspect was sitting. Concealed in the suspect's underwear, the missing beeper was rattling and vibrating against the metal chair.

"Once that pager went off, it was a little hard for the girl to keep denying she had it," Shepler says, "so that case was soon cleared."